P9-DDX-577

"Acknowledged as one of America's leading authorities on Christian higher education, David L. McKenna masterfully bridges the history of the movement in its quest for the integration of faith and learning. His insights provide a grateful affirmation of God's faithfulness and build a foundation for our future ringing deep and true. *Christ Centered Higher Education* will have a prominent place in my library."

—CHARLES H. WEBB,
President, Spring Arbor University

"Amazingly specific historical notes and insights. Ends with a new vision to guide the way. What a gift this will be."

—ROBERT ANDRINGA,
President Emeritus, Council for Christian Colleges and Universities

"This is extremely well written . . . I commend [this book as] another wonderful statement for those of us who continue to lead the way for Christian higher education."

—PHIL EATON,
President, Seattle Pacific University

"I . . . applaud as loudly as I am able the book's key message, that Christian colleges and universities should be eager to celebrate God's call to wholeness in Christ as the foundational premise of their work in providing collegiate-level education for all of God's human creation."

—RICHARD STEPHENS,
President Emeritus, Greenville College

"Combining intellectual autobiography with a penetrating analysis and critique of the plight of higher education, McKenna offers a powerful overview of the forces at work shaping our universities and colleges as they, in turn, shape each new generation of students . . . Beyond the numerous insights sprinkled throughout the book, the analysis of the evolution of higher education in America is one of the most riveting and provocative of any available."

—GAYLE D. BEEBE,
President, Westmont College

"I found this a great read with so much resonance with my own life's purpose . . . I already have a list of people to whom I want to give this book."

—GEORGE BRUSHABER,
President Emeritus, Bethel University

Christ-Centered Higher Education

Christ-Centered Higher Education

Memory, Meaning, and Momentum
for the Twenty-First Century

DAVID L. MCKENNA

 CASCADE *Books* · Eugene, Oregon

CHRIST-CENTERED HIGHER EDUCATION
Memory, Meaning, and Momentum for the Twenty-First Century

Cascade Books
An Imprint of Wipf and Stock Publishers
199 W. 8th Ave., Suite 3
Eugene, OR 97401

www.wipfandstock.com

ISBN 13: 978-1-62032-187-4

Cataloging-in-Publication data:

McKenna, David L.

Christ-centered higher education : memory, meaning, and momentum for the twenty-first century / David L. McKenna.

xx + 162 p. ; 23 cm. —Includes bibliographical references.

ISBN 13: 978-1-62032-187-4

1. Church and education — United States. 2. Christian universities and colleges — United States — History. I. Title.

LC383 .M323 2012

Manufactured in the U.S.A.

DEDICATED TO:

PRESENTS

Past, Present, Future

Who

See the vision,
State the mission,
and
Set the tone

for

Christ-centered higher education

Keynote
Center of Centers

"He is the image of the invisible God, the firstborn over all creation.
For by him all things were created;
things in heaven and on earth,
visible and invisible,
whether thrones or power
or rulers or authorities;
all things were created by Him and for Him.
He is before all things, and in Him all things hold together."

Colossians 1:15-17 (N.I.T)

Contents

Part 4: Sustaining Momentum

Foreword

FORGETFULNESS NEVER SERVES US well. We live in a culture that worships what's new, what's latest, what's on the cutting edge.

Interestingly, the Scriptures encourage us to remember, be mindful, know the story of what has gone before us. In other words, there is more to the story than what's new.

Of all the institutions started by the church, colleges and universities should be the best at remembering. The curriculum at all strong institutions includes courses in remembering. Courses in history, literature, the humanities, and religion are just a few of the foundational requirements of a healthy and robust educational experience. From different angles and different lenses they, if taught well, help us remember and contextualize our current story in the larger human story. They help us remember, lest we forget. They help inspire our vision, lest we make the same mistakes. They help us build on the lessons of the past, lest our vision for the future be held captive by the present.

David McKenna provides us, with this work, an important reminder for such a time as this. The Christian colleges and universities of today are in the midst of a time of significant change. The culture is changing. The institution of higher education is changing. Change is all around us. In the midst of this change, Dr. McKenna gives a personal glimpse into a pivotal half century of Christian higher education and does so in a manner that is self-reflective, prophetic, and celebratory.

The stories he weaves and tells are full of wisdom, confession, challenge, and hope. With the characteristic joy for which he has always been known, Dr. McKenna sets an important context for Christian higher education that trustees, faculty, administrators, and alumni would be wise to

absorb, particularly as a whole generation of leaders are retiring and passing the baton of leadership on to the next generation.

Like a true Wesleyan, Dr. McKenna draws from Scripture, tradition,
reason, and experience. But his is not a stale memoir or boring theological
treatise. It is the story of a faithful pilgrim seeking to follow his Lord and
"work it out with fear and trembling."

N. T. Wright has recently observed that "what finally changes the
world right now is flesh—words with skin on them. Words that hug you
and cry with you; words that play with you and love you; words that rebuke
you and eat with you. Words with flesh on them remain the most powerful
force in the world!"

While there are many wise insights and helpful lessons to be gained
from this work, these two anchor truths permeate Dr. McKenna's thoughts
and become the unifying themes of this book: **Incarnation** and **Ideas**.

Incarnation Matters. If Christian higher education is going to make a
difference in the next half-century and beyond, it will be because everyone
who has any part in the enterprise remembers, "The word became flesh
and dwelt among us." Incarnation matters. Incarnation is not only an astounding theological claim, it is the most powerful of all pedagogical and
leadership principles.

Ideas Matter. One of Dr. McKenna's fellow Scotsmen, Andrew Fletch-
er, once remarked, "Give me the songs of a nation and it does not matter
who writes its laws." Christian educators *have* to care about ideas—the ways
in which ideas are nurtured and communicated. Of course ideas and incarnation are intimately related, and in this story that President McKenna
weaves, we see them come together in ways to which we can relate.

The colleges and universities about which students, parents, and all
other constituencies will rise up and call blessed are those where lives are
changed through a transformational learning experience in the midst of
an authentic and vibrant campus community. These communities will take
shape in dozens of diverse and new ways, utilizing the rapidly changing
methodologies that are unfolding in our day; but they will all have the
"DNA" of incarnation and be lovers of ideas with Kingdom implications.

David McKenna, one of the "tribal elders" of Christian higher education, has done us a great service in the telling of these stories and "connecting the dots" of the recent past of the people, institutions, and movements
of Christ-centered learning of recent decades in North America.

Let those who will, have ears to hear. Let all who dare, move forward boldly to become the thousand points of light he calls for and move to light the way to a fruitful future.

We are all indebted to David McKenna for telling this story. We are even more indebted to Dr. McKenna and the hundreds of other leaders, named and unnamed, who faithfully and sacrificially stewarded this movement throughout the generations and season of the last half of the 20th century.

Our single prayer should be: Long may their tribes increase.

Steve Moore
2012

Acknowledgments

JOHN WESLEY SAID, "THERE is no such thing as a solitary Christian." The same truth applies to the writer of a book. There is no such thing as a solitary author. A host of persons contribute to our writing. Some are lost to memory, others are vividly present in our mind's eye at the present moment. In the dedication, I acknowledged colleagues in the presidency who took leadership in forming the Christian College Consortium at the national level while advancing the integration of faith and learning on their individual campuses. Story after story could be written about each of them, whom I knew and from whom I learned. Their names write a bold and glorious chapter in the history of Christ-centered higher education.

After completing the first draft of this book, I asked some of our past and present leaders if they would read what I wrote, check the accuracy, critique the text, and assess the tone. Sometimes a request like this is as hollow as a casual "How are you?" to a stranger on the street. We ask the question, but we don't want to know the answer. In this case, however, there was an urgent need to hear the answer because memoirs often carry the kiss of death in publication. So, I dared to ask each of them the question, "Does the book come off as self-serving?" In my own mind, I had already decided that I would never ask the book to be published if it smacked the least of that message.

As always, my colleagues came through. Suggestions for revision of both text and tone set me writing again. Their memories enlarged the picture and made connections in areas that I had missed. Their sharp eyes caught sentences or paragraphs that could be misinterpreted. Their honesty took me back to rereading the text in order to seek the delicate balance among the critical elements of a personal story, institutional history, and a transformational movement. The result is far from perfect, but thanks to them, the story can now be told. I am especially indebted to: Robert Andringa, President Emeritus of the Council for Christian Colleges & Universities; Richard Stevens, President Emeritus of Greenville College; George Brushaber, President Emeritus of Bethel University; Phil Eaton, President Emeritus of the Seattle Pacific University; Stan Gaede, President of the Christian College Consortium; and Steve Moore, President/Executive Director of the Murdock Trust, who so graciously wrote the foreword for the book.

Archivists are people whom I especially admire. While some might think that sorting through dusty files and reading old documents is the most boring work in the world, I see archivists serving to keep our community of memory alive so that a new generation doesn't have to reinvent the wheel or repeat the errors of the past. Special appreciation goes to Joyce King, Secretary to the President at Seattle Pacific University, whose foresight led her to preserve presidential papers that would have been lost; Donald Bowell, Archivist for Consortium of Christian College documents at Taylor University; Adrienne Meir, University Archivist at Seattle Pacific University; Grace Yoder, Archivist and Special Collections Librarian at Asbury Theological Seminar;, and Susan Panak, University Archivist at Spring Arbor University. Each of these persons responded promptly and professionally to any request that I made of them. Their commitment to preserve the history of their institutions and the movement of Christ-centered higher education is a ministry worthy of recognition and honor.

At home, I have the best of resident critics and consultants in our four children and their spouses. Douglas, retired Microsoft executive coach, will not let me wander too far from sound leadership theory; Debra, our law school professor and trustee at Spring Arbor University and Asbury Theological Seminary, assures the intellectual property; Suzanne, Senior Human Resources Director at Microsoft, watches over relationships, and Robert, Chair of Industrial/Organizational Psychology at Seattle Pacific University, doublechecks for spiritual integrity. Their spouses multiply these gifts. Kimberly wields the sharpest of red pencils, Ed handles political sensitivities, Scott adds the strategic perspective, and Jackie always sees the bright side. Thanks to them for speaking the truth with love.

Of course, when love is mentioned, every book I have ever written should be dedicated to Jan, my wife of more than 62 years. I can never forget that she gave up a career as one of the very best of elementary school teachers in order to be First Lady on three campuses for the next 33 years.

Now, in retirement, she lets me spend hours at the computer during the week, but draws the line on Friday when it is "Date Night." Neither words, songs, poetry nor flowers can ever let her know how much I owe her for the gift of unconditional love.

Introduction
Momentum for a Movement

WHEN PETER DRUCKER SPOKE, everybody listened. We paid particular attention when he made the pronouncement, "*The most significant sociological phenomenon of the second half of the 20th century has been the development of the large pastoral church—of the megachurch. It is the only organization that is actually working in our society.*" [1]

Who dares to counter Peter Drucker? The megachurch *is* a rare phenomenon born in the twentieth century that is still gaining momentum today. At the same time, I contend that its significance is matched by the renaissance in Christian higher education that also took place in the second half of the twentieth century. The story of this rebirth may be even more astounding because an existing institution, not a start-up organization, went through the rare process of transformational change. Beginning in mid-century as an endangered species on the edge of survival, the sector finished the era as an empowered partner in American higher education with a global outreach. Common cause and unprecedented cooperation among Christ-centered colleges and universities is a phenomenon that matches the megachurch as we move forward into the twenty-first century.

Such a transformation seldom takes place in a moment of time. A social movement with momentum is identified by four thrusts. First, against the odds, it *creates space* for transformational change. Second, around a commanding truth, it generates a *critical mass* for cooperative action around a commanding truth. Third, energized by that truth, it moves forward with *gathering speed*. Fourth, in order to *sustain its momentum*, it envisions moving forward into new space with greater impact at a higher level.

1. Rick Warren quoting Peter Drucker at the Pew Forum on Religion and Public Life, May 23, 2005.

The plan for this book is to tell the story of these four thrusts in the movement of Christian higher education on a timeline running from mid-twentieth century into the second decade of the twenty-first century. Part I walks us through the wrenching steps of "**Creating Space**" that Christian higher education took in order to be open to the prospects of transformational change. Despite dire predictions of its death at the beginning of the twentieth century, the sector laid claim to its divine mission, refused to die, took advantage of environmental shifts, followed its leaders, and made its own shift from a defensive posture to an affirming future. Part II, "**Generating Mass**," opens with the visionary call to promising options for Christian higher education, proceeds to a formative gathering for institutional cooperation, finds its common cause in the commanding truth of integrating faith and learning, sketches the start-up years of the Christian College Consortium, and attends the birth of the Christian College Coalition as a cohesive and effective force. Part III, "**Gathering Speed**," then offers reflective insights into the turning points, pivotal questions, and energizing motives that have made Christian higher education a movement with momentum. Finally, Part IV, "**Sustaining Momentum**," pulls together the insights of the past and points forward to the next level of impact for Christ-centered colleges and universities in the church, the academy, and the globe.

Can the story of transformational change be told from the perspective of an observer as well as a participant? Presumably, an observer writes objective history while a participant records personal memoirs. The division is artificial. In transformational change, especially when the Spirit of God is at work, observers of history cannot be separated from participants in the story. I write, *Christ-centered Higher Education: Memory, Meaning, and Momentum for the 21st Century*, from experience as well as history, from fact as well as perception, from grace as well as truth, and from heart as well as the head. Consequently, the text will blend scholarly research, personal participation, reflective insights, and future hopes.

I am eager to write the story because I lived through so many of the happenings. My purpose is not self-serving. I do not consider myself a pioneer, founder or head of the movement of Christ-centered higher education. Rather, I see myself as part of the team of Consortium of Christian College presidents who are acknowledged throughout this book and honored in Appendix B. With them and for them, I write as a colleague given the privilege of being involved first-hand in the making of a movement and living long enough to tell the story for our community of memory in

Christ-centered higher education. But, I cannot stay with memory alone.
My all-consuming passion is to write for trustees, presidents, deans, and
professors of today and tomorrow who carry forward the legacy of meaning and momentum for the integration of faith and learning. Out of this
group, my hearts beats as one with the next generation of presidents for
Christ-centered colleges and universities. If, in any way, this book helps to
identify, develop, and encourage them, its highest purpose will be met. To
these emerging leaders, I dedicate this book and ask that they join me in
singing the prayer:

> May the mind of Christ my Savior
> Live in me from day to day,
> By His love and power controlling
> All I do and say.
>
> May His beauty rest upon me
> As I seek the lost to win,
> And may they forget the channel
> Seeing only Him.[2]

Humbled by his Spirit and with future generations in mind, I invite you to
read the story of rebirth in Christian higher education through the eyes of
a participating observer. Forget the channel and see only him.

2. "May the Mind of Christ, My Savior," text by Kay B. Wilkinson and music by A.
Cyril Barham-Gould.

PART 1

Creating Space

"A movement begins when leaders with imagination see space for transformational change."

1

Endangered Species

If the Christian college did not exist, would it have to be invented? Senti-ment gives an impassioned "Yes!" to this question, but scholarship requires us to ask, "If so, why?" This book is a mix of sentiment and scholarship. In 1947 I answered "Yes!" as a freshman at a Christian college and in that love affair I found my calling and my career. Later, as a PhD candidate in the Center for the Study of Higher Education at the University of Michigan, leading scholars in American higher education challenged me to answer the question, "Why?"

Sixty years later sentiment and scholarship come together. After com-pleting my PhD in the administration of higher education, I immersed myself in the movement of Christian higher education as a professor, dean, president, board chair, and consultant for executive search and board gov-ernance. Based upon these credentials and the perspective of time, I make my claim as a witness to rebirth in Christ-centered higher education during the second half of the twentieth century, with the momentum of a trans-formative movement that will make it indispensable to the Kingdom in the twenty-first century. But first, the story of an endangered species.

AN OMINOUS BEGINNING

The nineteenth century might well be called "the Century of Defection" for Christian higher education. In the opening years of the 1800s Christian colleges and universities joined in the leadership of spiritual awakening and social reform as American democracy made it way West under the aegis, "One nation under God." Two-thirds of the way through the century, however, forces within the culture and the academy undercut these spiritual moorings. German Enlightenment, in particular, captured the minds of faculty in many colleges and universities that had moorings in Christian faith. With empirical reason expelling biblical revelation, the defection began. By the end of the nineteenth century, most of the colleges that had led the way in the Christian liberal arts and spiritual renewal had either modified or abandoned their faith position so that the name "Christian" had meaning only as an historical artifact.

The twentieth century opened on a note of irony. At the same time that the lofty promises of the social gospel were pointing to "The Christian Century," colleges and universities who held a faith position were predicted to die a merciful death on a short time span. William Rainey Harper, President of the University of Chicago, wrote *The Trend in Higher Education*, in 1905, with the most dire view of the future for these colleges.[1] Surveying the educational landscape of the Midwest, a mecca for small denominational colleges, he bluntly wrote that only 25 percent of them had a chance to survive. The other 75 percent were destined to mediocrity or slow death.

Harper backed up with his prediction with six observations. First, the rapid development of public high schools would result in "people's colleges" that duplicated the offerings of the Christian college. Second, the demand for vocational specialization would cancel the perceived value of the liberal arts curriculum. Third, the societal trend away from the narrow sectarian spirit toward a broader, ecumenical outlook undercut the *raison d'etre* of denominational colleges. Fourth, the rapid expansion and rising prestige of the public university would weaken the appeal of the small religious college. Fifth, competition with the public university for faculty would leave the small college recruiting either the very new and inexperienced or the very old and second-rate scholars. Sixth, and most serious, Harper saw limited financial resources against rising costs as the nail in the coffin of the small Christian college. Hidden behind these charges were the unspoken issues from the academic community denying the intellectual validity of the Christian college because of the alleged lack of academic freedom in scholarship, the indoctrination of students in teaching, the repressive domination of *in loco parentis*, and the ecclesiastical control of leadership

1. Harper, *The Trend of Higher Education*, 349ff.

through presidents who were ordained clergy. Without the slightest show of mercy, Harper sounded the death knell on Christian colleges by pronouncing, "Death in these cases is of course a blessing—not only to the institutions that have died, but to the world around them."[2] With that indictment ringing in its ears, the small Christian college stepped into the twentieth century.

SURVIVAL INSTINCTS

William Rainey Harper didn't live to eat his words. But, if he had lived, he would have been pressed to admit that he was wrong, not just about the survival rate of these colleges, but about the start-up rate of new institutions with Christian identity. Even though some of his six predictions came true, such as limited resources and rising costs, he forgot four sharp tools in the survival kit for Christian colleges.

First, President Harper missed the love that holds the Christian college together. As a historian, he should have remembered Daniel Webster's defense of Dartmouth College before the Supreme Court in 1816. Against the State's contention that all American higher education should be public, Webster successfully carried the case for Dartmouth as a self-governing and independent institution with a mission distinctive from the public sector. Webster closed his case with these words to Chief Justice John Marshall, "As I had said earlier, Mr. Chief Justice, the college may be small, but there are those who love her."[3] Yes, there is a love that will not let the Christian college go.

Second, Harper failed to see the discipline of sacrifice in Christian colleges. Through thick and thin, trustees, administrators, faculty, and alumni will make sacrifices of love for the institutions that have nurtured them, intellectually and spiritually. In contrast to institutions that go to the public trough in financial crisis, Christian colleges are disciplined in making the most out of limited resources. In crisis, they tighten their belt another notch. Moreover, the depth of love among alumni, denominational members, ethnic families, and local communities is tapped in times of need.

This fact is very personal with me. When my wife Janet and I arrived to take the presidency of Seattle Pacific College in 1968, severe financial

2. Ibid., 376.

3. Daniel Webster, Oral Argument before the Supreme Court of the United States, March 10, 1818, in Dartmouth vs. Woodward case.

crisis threatened our credibility in the academy as well as the community. In August, while waiting for the influx of tuition dollars, we did not have the funds to meet payroll and our line of credit with the bank had been exhausted. Radical budgets adjustments would have to be made, debts consolidated, and creditors convinced to give us time to pay our bills. But when the word reached the churches of our small denomination, sacrificial giving stemmed the tide. One letter in our permanent collection comes from a member of a small Free Methodist Church in Oregon, "I am sending you the savings from my Christmas Club to help out." This is not an isolated incident. Every Christian college that has faced financial crisis can tell the same story.

Third, Harper overlooked the sense of divine calling behind the existence of the Christian college. When consulting with the board of a Christian college, I often open with this challenge, "The board of trustees of a Christian college should begin every meeting with the motion to discontinue the school, dissolve the corporation, and disperse the assets." This is another way of asking our leading question, "If the Christian college did not exist, would it have to be invented?" Only when the ensuing debate brings the trustees back to the reason for their existence should the meeting continue.

Read the history of Christian colleges. Invariably, the founders claim that the institution is ordained of God and indispensable to his mission on earth. Admittedly, this conviction has a dark side. Some Christian colleges are founded for the wrong purposes and kept on life support long after they have should have expired. Colleges die hard and Christian colleges die harder.

Early-twentieth-century history shows few Christian colleges dying and many more being started, such as Azusa, Westmont, and Biola. In each case, the call of God to an indispensable mission stood behind these life and death decisions.

Fourth, President Harper's most meaningful misjudgment came when he failed to see the integration of faith and learning as the distinctive contribution of Christian higher education to American culture. Stranger than fiction, William Rainey Harper excelled in teaching Hebrew, Greek, and Old Testament. Yet, somehow, he missed the connection between his scholarship and the question out of which the university system was originally formed, "What has Jerusalem to do with Athens?" If he had asked that question he would have had to consider the fact that the Christian college was the only institution of higher education that existed exclusively to answer it. However imperfect or impoverished the Christian college might have been, its contribution to the dialogue could not be denied. At the very least it stood a as reminder of the original question that great institutions such as Harper's University of Chicago had either dismissed or forgotten. Moreover, when push came to shove, the integration of faith and learning gave the Christian college its holding power against the rising tide of a secular culture and a humanistic educational system.

LIVING THE STORY

My introduction to Christian higher education included all four of these survival tools. College was not in my plans until I sensed the call to ministry as a high school junior. Out of a non-college family and an anti-college church, everyone expected me to go to a Bible school. My search through college catalogs, however, introduced me to Taylor University and Marion College.

One Saturday, my parents drove me to Indiana to look at these schools. Nothing clicked so we headed home. On the way through Coldwater, Michigan, my mother asked to see if we could find a grocery store where she could be a buy a roast for Sunday. In the center of town, she spotted Reppert's Market and went in. My father and I followed. While scouting out the store, I noticed no alcohol or tobacco. Then, I saw a card on the meat counter announcing a revival with Reverend Harry Hosmer, in the local Free Methodist Church. Turning to my father, I said, "Dad, this must be a Christian store." No sooner were the words out of my mouth when the front door opened and the evangelist whose picture was on the card walked in, followed by a young man in a high school varsity jacket. Dad walked over to the evangelist, introduced himself, and said that he remembered going to Ypsilanti High School with the reverend's sister.

They started reminiscing when my mother interrupted, "We are looking for a Christian college for our son." The young man in the varsity jacket, the evangelist's son with the same name, lighted up and asked, "Have you considered Spring Arbor Junior College?" We confessed that we had never heard of the school. Harry, Jr., a gifted salesman and student at the College, urged us to drive up M-60 from Coldwater rather than continuing on US-12 to Ypsilanti. By the time we arrived at the campus, a brilliant moon shone upon a cluster of buildings with its brightest beam outlining the first floor of a new dormitory under construction. Sixty-three years later, my memory of that moment sparkles with clarity. Spring Arbor Junior College was the place where God had led us and to which He was calling me.

Final confirmation came at freshman orientation when I heard the President declare Spring Arbor Junior College "a vine of God's own planting," and the Director of Alumni tell the story of Bishop E. P. Hart and his wife, pioneer founders of the school. As they got off the train in 1873 at the Spring Arbor whistle stop, Mrs. Hart peered through driving snow at the distant tracks and declared, "As long as there is a track, we will never turn back." Then, together we rose to sing the school song,

> There is a place 'twill ne'er be forgot,
> far dearer than lake or pine.
> So speed the glad and the chorus prolong,
> 'Til the echoes reach heaven above,
> Spring Arbor the school we love.

Later that same afternoon, I began my work as a student laborer to pay my college costs. Shoveling mud in a drainage ditch, my fellow digger introduced himself as Clarence DeCan, Director of Finance and Controller for the College.

As grand as these memories may be, the brightest of shining moments were reserved for my intellectual awakening when professors grappled with the implications of their faith for the conceptual, moral, and social issues rising out of their fields of study. For the first time, I heard the words of the hymn that Charles Wesley wrote for the inauguration of John Wesley's Kingswood School in Kingswood, England:

> Unite the pair so long disjoined,
> Knowledge and vital piety;
> Learning and love combined,
> And Truth and love, let all men see,
> In those who up to Thee we give,
> Thine, wholly Thine, to die and live.[4]

As the product of a fundamentalist church in a black and white world, I came alive with a thirst for knowledge that would take me to the highest of academic degrees. My path of learning may look like the tracks of a crab waddling from side to side through majors in history, theology, psychology, and higher education. Looking back, however, the direction never changed.

4. Wesley, Wesley and Osborn, *The Poetical Works of John and Charles Wesley*, 408.

In a Christian college targeted for extinction, I took the first step in the will of God toward the goal of integrating my biblical faith in Jesus Christ with an unquenchable thirst for life-long learning.

2

Substitute Sanctuary

AMERICAN HIGHER EDUCATION TOOK on the role as savior of a democratic society at the opening of the second half of the twentieth century. When the hopes and plans for reconstruction after World War II were formulated, a messianic vision for our colleges and universities led the way. Without the slightest hesitation, political and academic leaders spoke about the "democratic faith" with public institutions serving as sanctuaries where the faith would be taught by the high priests of the faculty and learned by the student parishioners in the classroom. Never before or since has American higher education savored such public confidence or promised such idealistic results.

A NEW REVELATION

Harry Truman's Presidential Commission on Higher Education wrote the book of revelation for this new American dream. Under the title of *Higher Education for American Democracy,* the report cast the vision of an "expansive, inclusive, and diverse" system of public higher education that would assure access and opportunity for every young person in the nation.[1] To achieve this goal, tuition-free "people's colleges" or "community colleges" were proposed for every state in the Union, even going so far as to envision

1. Brubacher and Rudy, *Higher Education in Transition,* 230–32

one within commuting distance for every student in state. With equality of access came the plan for equality of opportunity as provided by a massive program of financial aid so that no student could be denied because of lack of funds. To further assure diversity, special consideration was given to gender for women and race for African Americans.

A new definition of General Education served as the core of the vision to replace scattershots in curriculum development. At one extreme, the classical liberal arts with its emphasis upon freeing the mind got tagged as aristocratic. At the other extreme, the ever-expanding vocational and technical curricula received the criticism of being a cafeteria or smorgasbord of disparate offerings. For all public schools, whether community college or national university, the Truman Commission recommended a General Education in the first and second years of college that would lead the student to understand the meaning of freedom in the democratic faith. On this foundation, then, the student would work to resolve the issues of the democratic enterprise and join in association with all of the members of the global community.[2] Secular idealists have their own version of integrating faith and learning.

How did Christian colleges fit into the vision? For the most part, they were ignored. The Truman Commission did not expect private sector enrollments to grow even though it included their college students under the plan for financial aid. Heated arguments followed as Protestant and Catholic educators feared total government take-over through the conduit of student financial aid. By inference, at least, the report of the Commission assumed that private colleges had little to contribute to the ideals of equal access and equal opportunity in fulfilling the American dream. In addition, the proposal of the Report for a standard curriculum in General Education appeared to undermine the classical liberal arts of distinguished private colleges as aristocratic. Even more significantly, the idea of making democratic faith the center for integration in human learning stood in direct opposition to the integration of Christian faith and human learning in the Christian college. Perhaps critics of the Commission overstated their case, but once again they heard the sounds of the death knell for a majority of private institutions in the nation. Once again, it proved to be false alarm, but not without consequences for the Christian college. Already discredited as inferior by the academic community at the start of the century, it now had to deal with a political climate in which it was considered irrelevant.

2. Ibid.

A PERSONAL ENCOUNTER

At the height of the fervor created by the Truman Commission in 1953, I entered the scene as a Dean of Men and designated hitter for teaching courses in religion, psychology, English, and speech at my alma mater, Spring Arbor Junior College and Academy. A sharp turn in the road of my career path led me to the position.

After completing a Bachelor of Arts degree in History at Western Michigan University, I enrolled at Asbury Theological Seminary in Wilmore, Kentucky to pursue a Master of Divinity degree, with plans for a future in pastoral ministry. While there, however, the latent impulse for intellectual pursuits came to life through my interest in clinical pastoral psychology and I began searching for PhD programs in that field. In the spring of 1953, just prior to my graduation from seminary, I had been accepted for doctoral study at both Boston University and the University of Southern California. To support our young family, a parish awaited on the East Coast and I held a contract for teaching religion at our small denominational college on the West Coast. Although I felt suspended between options, one thing was clear: A PhD was my highest priority. I would make a career in Christian higher education rather than pastoral ministry.

A chapel service on campus became the turning point in my life. Our guest speaker was Dr. J. T. Seamands, a long-term missionary in India. His address followed a pattern that I had heard from missionary speakers time after time, with one exception. Instead of asking his congregation to answer God's call with the general commitment, "Here am I, send me," he said, "India needs you now. Who is willing to go?" Even though I felt as if he were speaking directly to me, I did not go forward because India was not in my plans. But, as I left chapel, Dr. Seamands' call kept coming back with my name on it. I was paralyzed and could not go on until the issue was settled.

Kneeling at the bedside in our small apartment, I entered my own Gethsemane. Time got lost in the hour or two that I argued with God, "Why would you lead me so far along the path toward the PhD and then change your mind?" God did not have to answer. I knew that I was caught in a battle of wills with eternal consequences. Would I do the will of God and go to India or would I do my own will and get the PhD? Tracing back through other turning points in my spiritual journey, I knew that God had never led me astray when I vowed to do his will. So, with full and final resolution, I told God, "If You want me to go to India, I will go even if I never get a PhD."

Fifty-seven years later, skeptical minds will ask, "Why do you have a PhD but you've never been to India?" I have no answer other than to cite the story of Abraham and Isaac. Just as God asked Abraham to sacrifice Isaac as a test of wills, God asked me to give up the PhD and go to India in order to win my will. Once the decision was made, however, the path to a PhD came clear. The President of Spring Arbor Junior College called to invite me to a position, my application for graduate studies at the University of Michigan was readily accepted. And in all of the years that have followed, I stand ready to go to India at a moment's notice.

FAITH TO FAITH

These movements in my life were amplified by their alignment with deeper, wider currents flowing in higher education. By going to Spring Arbor Junior College and enrolling for graduate work at the University of Michigan, I learned that the University had established the first program in the nation for doctoral studies preparing students for college presidencies. It was a dream come true. Even more remarkable was the fact that the Director of the newly established Center for the Study of Higher Education, first in the nation, was Dr. Algo D. Henderson, one of the most prominent members of the Truman Commission on Higher Education in American Democracy. His background included being a lead architect for the New York State University System of Higher Education and President of Antioch College, known as an experimental college combining work and study with students who were both creative and edgy.

Dr. Henderson and I made an odd couple for the study of American higher education. In our first meeting, he informed me that he was an agnostic and a liberal. At the same time, he acknowledged my faith and appreciated the fact that Christians made the best graduate students because they were eager to learn and open to other views while holding their own. Every course that I took from Dr. Henderson, ranging from the history and philosophy to curriculum to administration in higher education, began and ended with the ideals of the Truman Commission Report. The passion with which he taught left no doubt. Dr. Henderson was a prime architect for the Report. His teaching was complemented by courses from the most prominent professors in the field of American higher education, such as John Siler Brubacher, co-author of the eminent history *Higher Education in America,* and M. M. Chambers, chronicler of issues and trends in higher education.

Personal time with Dr. Henderson became the unexpected bonus for graduate studies. He invited me to meetings with visiting scholars, such as Lewis Mayhew, champion of the small liberal arts college, and national names in higher education, including Earl McCrath, John Dale Russell, Clark Kerr and others. Under his tutelage, I wrote and published articles in the *Journal of Liberal Education* and the *Junior College Journal.* On one occasion, Dr. Henderson and his wife, Anne, set up dinner for Janet and me at the home of Harlan Hatcher, President of the University of Michigan to advance the cause of the Center for the Study of Higher Education.

The experience proved priceless. As a young administrator in a small Christian college targeted for extinction, I learned first-hand about the philosophy, policies, and practices of American higher education, both historically and in the contemporary scene. Consequently, when I completed my degree and advanced to Dean and then Vice-President of Spring Arbor Junior College, I knew the field where the game was being played and I had an idea about how to win.

3

Paradigm Shift

AMERICAN HIGHER EDUCATION IS a faith-based enterprise held up by a three-legged stool. Each leg is labeled with specific meaning for "equality" in a democracy. One leg is the "equality of access" so that any person can become a student in a college or university. Another leg is the "equal of opportunity" so that any student can be assured of funding for higher education. The Report of the Truman Commission on American Democracy in Higher Education gave its primary attention to these two legs of the three-legged stool.

THE THIRD LEG

A two-legged stool cannot stand. To assure the vision of democracy in American higher education, the third leg of "equality of quality" among colleges and universities must be put in place. For good reason, the Truman Commission tread gently in this area. To realize the ideal of "equality of quality" would mean upsetting the vertical scale on which colleges and universities were ranked, with elitist institutions at the top. If quality were judged on a horizontal basis with the common denominator of General Education for Democracy in the curriculum, a local community college would be equal in quality to a national research university, just different in function. When the implications of *Higher Education for American Democracy* were spelled out in our classes at the University of Michigan, there was no doubt that the third leg was required to fulfill the dream. No wonder that the Truman Commission tread lightly on "equality of quality." To change the attitude of the academy toward the "equality of quality" would require a revolution. Could it ever be done?

THE SERPENTINE MONSTER

A vertical system of status in American higher education had to be toppled to realize the dream of the Truman Commission. In his book, *Constraint and Variety in American Education,* David Reisman, Harvard Professor of Sociology, created the image of American higher education as a serpentine monster standing up and slogging forward with a twisting, turning head, followed by a bloated middle body, and balanced on a torporific tail dragging on the ground behind.[1] Avant-garde institutions of academic prestige, led by Harvard, made up the head; public and regional universities gave bulk to the middle body; and small denominational schools joined with community colleges in the sluggish tail.

Reisman's low estimation of denominational schools showed itself in his statements that these institutions are "colleges only by the grace of semantic generosity,"[2] enrolling students whose "morals are more actively monitored than their minds,"[3] and "as the colleges 'above' them and the high schools 'below' them improve, they must also change or perish, though for a time they can hang on by catering to ever lower intellectual levels and aspirations."[4]

As the title of Reisman's book suggests, he is open to constraint and variety in American education as defined by elitist excellence. It is a contradiction in terms to talk about the "equality of excellence." Reisman's image of American higher education as a serpent with a twisting head, bloated body, and sluggish tail reinforces a vertical and comparative ranking of colleges and universities. But, as the Truman Commission envisioned, a revolution was on the way. The vertical scale tipped to the horizontal when the approach to accrediting institutions of higher education shifted from quantity toward quality in its standards.

1. Reisman, *Constraint and Variety in American Education,* 35ff.
2. Ibid., 61–62
3. Ibid.
4. Ibid.

PURPOSE-DRIVEN QUALITY

In the 1950s, the accrediting process ran counter to the ideal of "equality of quality" among institutions of higher education. As a system of self-regulation based upon peer evaluation, avant-garde schools set the standards. Even though, as Reisman admitted, educational institutions at the head of the academic procession are "often turning back upon themselves" with uncertainty as to direction or success.[5]

Such vacillation kept all of the other institutions in the serpentine body trying to stay in pace with darting and twisting motions of the head. Consequently, the standards for academic quality were so elusive that the accreditation on a vertical scale kept falling back upon quantitative judgments of dollars, degrees, books, and brains. With regret, we note this regression continuing to the current time when Christian colleges and universities tout their position on the *US News and World Report* ratings or defend their status on Department of Education assessments of academic quality based upon statistical quantity. We need to heed the wisdom attributed to Albert Einstein, "Not everything that can be counted counts, and not everything that counts can be counted."

VOLUNTARY SELF-REGULATION

In contrast with state-run systems controlling education, voluntary self-regulation is a crowning virtue of American colleges and universities. When educators themselves take on the responsibility for the assessment of quality in colleges and universities, good things happen. A quick-hitting history of accrediting in the 20th century tells us why.

A form of accreditation began in the first decade of the twentieth century when the Carnegie Foundation for the Advancement of Teaching funded pension plans for professors under the well-known acronym, TIAA-CREF. To qualify for the plan, however, the institutions had to meet such conditions as employing a minimum of six faculty members, offering a four-year program in arts and science, and requiring a high school diploma for admission. When the federal government made an attempt to enforce these educational standards, the North Central Association for Accreditation was formed as a voluntary, self-regulating agency for both secondary and higher education. Individual states also got into the act with

5. Ibid., 35.

accrediting agencies of their own. Then, when the lack of uniformity among regional and state agencies created greater confusion, the National Council for Accreditation became the coordinator for the system. Standardization, of course, has its own dark side in the tendency toward uniformity and conformity, especially when trying to establish measurable criteria for academic quality in all institutions. Whether coming from a Ministry of Education or a Department of Education, attempts to standardize learning outcomes tend to fall back upon quantitative standards.

After half a century of jostling between qualitative or quantitative standards, accrediting in the 1950s gave lip service to qualitative principles, but succumbed to quantitative practices. Though the hodge-podge of state, regional, and professional accrediting agencies was presumably coordinated by the National Council on Accrediting, quantitative measures created according to the benchmark of elitist institutions ruled the day. Size of the endowment, PhDs on the faculty, selectivity of students, GRE scores, and volumes in the library led the way in recognizing quality.

While some small Christian colleges had achieved accreditation in their regional areas, most of them continued to operate under the aegis of a state accrediting system that held less rigorous standards. In response to this evident need, the Council for the Advancement of Small Colleges was organized in 1955 for the specific purpose of assisting colleges with enrollments under 2,000 to achieve regional accreditation. After this initial thrust, the name was changed to the Council for Independent Colleges, with extended programs in governance and management for their members. The venture paid off.

As colleges strengthened their positions on quantitative criteria, accrediting agencies moved toward qualitative standards, and small colleges found a collective voice in the halls of Congress, a brighter future dawned for the Christian college. Tracing the shifts in the mindset of the academic community, no change is more significant than the shift from comparative quantity of resources to customized quality of purpose in the educational enterprise. In this change, Christian colleges found hope.

PROOF OF PURPOSE

As a case in point, when I began my career in 1953 at Spring Arbor Junior College, the enrollment topped out at 170 students, no faculty member held a terminal degree, the curriculum layered biblical courses with general education, the budget was balanced by a last minute gift from a loyal donor, and state accreditation rested uneasily on the legitimacy of a legal charter and the generosity of a visiting team.

When I inherited the position as Academic Dean of the Junior College in 1956, the school enjoyed accredited status with the Michigan Commission on College Accreditation. The recognition assured our students transfer status with other Michigan institutions and federal funding for veterans who chose Spring Arbor as the college of their choice.

Just a year after my appointment as Academic Dean for the junior college, however, word came from the Michigan Commission on College Accreditation, now chaired by Algo Henderson, my advisor and mentor at the University of Michigan, that our accredited status with the state would be canceled unless we achieved significant progress toward North Central regional accreditation within the next two years.

Ordinarily, this would be cause for institutional panic. But, Dr. Henderson, my mentor, had taught me well. In order to demonstrate the democratic ideal at work in American higher education, he toppled the vertical scale of competitive academic quality and laid it on a horizontal plane where educational quality was defined by consistency, not comparison. Rather than looking down upon "lesser" institutions, each institution held its own esteem in the educational system according to its defined purpose, whether vocational programs in two-year colleges or doctoral programs in research universities. Accreditation followed this model. In the simplest scheme, quality in a college or university was to be determined by the clarity and consistency of its purpose, program, and product backed up by sufficient resources to do the job.

The "show cause" notice from the Michigan College Commission with the mandate to gain regional accreditation or lose all recognition cleared our minds and focused our attention. On quantitative criteria, the two-year probationary period did not give us enough time to build all of the resources required for regional accreditation. But, if we could show the clarity and consistency of our purpose, program, and product with significant gains in resources, we might have a chance. So, allying ourselves with the idealist model of quality in American higher education, we developed the plan for a self-study that would show Spring Arbor Junior College moving toward its role as a contributing member of our society. Our purpose was defined by the opportunity for students who wanted two years of Christian higher education before: (1) transferring to other institutions; (2) entering the job market; or (3) serving in Christian ministries. A revision of the curriculum provided a general education in the humanities, natural science, social science, philosophy, and religion for all students, along with special tracks for each category of student. Alumni studies were done to show successful products for our three-fold purpose. In support of this plan, our educational resources in faculty, finance and facilities were assessed in order to create a long-term plan for improvement.

We held our breath when the visiting team came to the campus, but then sighed with relief as they commended our self-study and granted us full regional accreditation as a two-year college with a follow-up review after a period of years to monitor our progress.

Our strenuous exercise in self-study for the board, administration, and faculty caught the front edge of a paradigm in American higher education. Emphasis upon qualitative criteria for academic recognition according to an integrated purpose, program, and product would become the standard for recognition in accrediting. With the change, Christian colleges could compete and reclaim their rightful place in American higher education. Such a shift, however, does not take place all at once. Like all transforming ideas, it takes the test of time to come to maturity.

4

Fragmented Fellowship

CHRISTIAN COLLEGES, IN THE MID-TWENTIETH century, were their own worst enemy. While gaining a measure of respect in the academic community through the revolutionary change in accrediting standards, among ourselves we nursed a low sense of self-esteem that found expression in fragmentation, competition, and defensiveness.

SPLINTERED SPIRIT

Fragmentation showed itself in a lack of cooperation among our colleges. Theological, denominational, and regional differences split the sector wide apart. When the National Association of Evangelicals came into being in the 1950s as a counterforce to fundamentalism and liberalism, the organization included a Commission on Christian Higher Education. Few college representatives attended and those who did quickly divided on such grounds as mission, theology, curriculum, and student standards. Some denominational colleges, for instance, saw their mission exclusively in serving the church and preparing its ministry. Calvinist schools faced off against Wesleyan schools. Bible colleges charged Christian liberal arts colleges of compromising on the Truth, and Christian liberal arts colleges countered with the claim that Bible colleges were out of touch with changing educational needs.

Some schools required faculty to sign strict statements of faith on an annual basis; others simply asked if faculty had any reservations on the theological position. Campus codes with varying degrees of restriction on student life discouraged any interaction, transfer, or cooperative ventures among the colleges.

At times, the competition became downright nasty as Christian college representatives pointedly bad-mouthed their competitors. My youthful idealism collided with these realities in a proposal that I made to the NAE Commission on Higher Education in 1959 for a national conference on Christian higher education where all of the schools could come together and work through their common and separate roles in fulfilling the Great Commission. The proposal died on the table for the want of a second.

I then tried my hand for cooperation at the denominational level. In the early 1960s, the Free Methodist Church of North America had seven Christian liberal arts colleges supported by 70,000 members in the United States, an average of 10,000 members per school. Two of the colleges, Greenville College (Illinois) and Roberts Wesleyan College (New York), were in the transition of presidents and the third, Spring Arbor Junior College, had announced plans to advance to four-year status.

Peering again through idealistic eyes, seeing the limited resources, and envisioning a momentous opportunity, I proposed that the three institutions come together, sell their campuses, and establish a Free Methodist university in Indianapolis. Bishops of the Church, Board Chairs of the colleges, and Chief Executive Officers of the institutions met together in Chicago to consider the proposal.

Reason pointed toward acceptance of the proposal, but emotion won the day. After the results were in, Bishop Charles Fairbairn, who carried the portfolio for Free Methodist Higher Education, concluded the meeting by saying to me, "David, you remind me of a little boy trying to throw water through a brick wall." Feeling spanked by his words, I left the meeting determined to show him that my institution, Spring Arbor College, would rise to equal or excel our competitors. I am not proud of that moment, but the bishop was right. A bucket of water does not bring down brick walls.

IRRECONCILABLE DIFFERENCES

If I had known what was happening in another Chicago hotel room during the same period, the bruising that I received from the Bishop would have been eased. In 1959, Carl Henry, editor of *Christianity Today,* proposed the establishment of an "evangelical Harvard" to counter the dominance of research and scholarship in public and secular institutions.[1] His proposal ignited the passion of Billy Graham as a partner in the project. Together, they invited evangelical leaders in theology, education, business, and philanthropy, including such names as Howard Butt, Stanley Kresge, Paul Harvey and Howard Pew, to come together with a view toward establishing a "Crusade University" at the highest level of academic excellence and stand out as the "citadel of Christian education."[2] Projected at a startup cost of $300 million, located at an urban center in proximity to a national research university, staffed by a faculty of "scholarly mentality," and supported by the best and brightest of student scholars in a climate of intellectual freedom, the new university was designed to meet a need not filled by existing Christian colleges.[3] Vigorous debate marked the meeting with divergence, not over theology or funding, but especially over location, standards of student morality, and whether or not the leaven of Christian scholarship would be lost in the secular university. Eventually, disagreement on the behavioral code for students divided the ranks and the meeting disbanded without action.

A year later, the group along with new members met again in New York City. Student morality still stymied the conversation and options for location of Crusade University divided the house. Eventually, these issues created a "quagmire" to which the businessmen said "No."[4] Out of the meeting, however, came the legacy of Carl Henry articulating the gold standard for the evangelical Christian university for his time and our future.

> More important than all considerations of "where and when,"
> however, is the basic matter of the image of this University and the
> academic world. Such a school, if worthy of its purpose, must deal
> with thought and life at their highest levels in the rich context of
> the Bible. It must be; *1) evangelical in urgency, 2) evangelical in doc-*
> *trine, 3) committed to academic standards and moral purity, but,*
> *unless it is much more also it cannot generally qualify as a Christian*
> *University.* Such an institution will not be too greatly interested
> in "the reputation of numbers," but *4) will honor the importance*

1. Owen Daniel Strachan, *Reenchanting the Evangelical Mind: Park Street Church's Harold Ockenga, The Boston Scholars, and the Mid-century Intellectual Surge,* 232.

2. Ibid.

3. Ibid., 243.

4. Ibid.

of personal academic relationships between professors and students.
Its qualified teachers must be concerned for *5) the unification of
all the university disciplines in the interest of a Christian world-life
view* which integrates the whole of life's experiences area with an
eye on tragic cultural crises of our times, they must *6) set forth the
political, economic and social applications of Christianity,* and thus
expound a consistent criticism of an alternative to socialistic revisions of the social order. Beyond a deep sense of personal devotion
to the Lord, the faculty must *7) grasp the history of thought and sys-
tematic orientation to Jesus Christ as the revealed center of history,
nature, conscience and redemption,* by bringing the "ancient mind,"
the "medieval mind," the "modern mind," the "contemporary
mind" under the judgment of divine revelation; besides interest
simply in personal projects and literary excursions, such a faculty
must be ready to *8) engage in corporate conversation, research and
writing,* each making some minimal contribution for the produc-
tion of textbooks that will enable the evangelical enterprise to
challenge the initiative of secular scholars, and to penetrate the
collegiate world. If such a university is really to rise to its greatest
potential, in its necessary dedication to evangelical standards of
doctrine of life, it will seek also to *9) provide a platform for the
ablest evangelical scholars of all traditions,* in order to solidify the
interdenominational, international witness of conservative Christianity.[5] (Emphases mine)

Henry held these nine imperatives with a conviction that caused him
to conclude, "It is my conviction that the surrender of any one of these
objectives will weaken the potential of a Christian university."[6]

Carl Henry never lost his dream for an "evangelical Harvard," but
he would be the first to understand if he had heard my story about trying to throw water through a brick wall. Sometimes the walls are man-
made, sometimes they are God-made, and sometimes you cannot tell the
difference.

FORTRESS MENTALITY

The low esteem of many evangelical Christian colleges showed itself most
clearly in a defensive outlook bordering on a fortress mentality. More often
than not, these schools got their identity by pushing off against secular and

5. Ibid., 260–61.
6. Ibid.

public institutions. While their mission statement did not come out and name the "devil with a face," their presentations for recruiting students, raising funds, or promoting the school carried the case against the evils of non-Christian higher education. Parents were warned against exposing their daughters to the moral cesspool of the public university. Presidents drew the contrast between the libertine public campus and the spiritual climate of their campus, where revivals broke out and every student received the invitation to come to Christ. Horror stories went out far and wide about Christian students being "tainted" by professors in secular and public universities.

I learned first-hand what they meant. During my first year of seminary I became interested in the developing field of clinical pastoral psychology. When I found a program at the University of Michigan offering courses in hospital chaplaincy I told my seminary advisor that I wanted to enroll and transfer graduate credit back to Master of Divinity degree. My request set in motion a series of conferences with professors who warned me about the subtle influence of liberal theology and Freudian psychology that would undermine my faith. Despite their protest, I took the first four-week intensive course and then enrolled for another four weeks of advanced study. During this time with students from seminaries of every theological stripe, we were forced into the process of "client-centered" or "non-directive" therapy with Carl Rogers and Seward Hilton as prophets of new truth. Episcopal students from a liberal seminary were the first to rebel when they insisted on reading scripture and praying with dying patients. Brought to alert, I decided to do an in-depth study of the assumptions behind the theory of Rogers and Hilton. To their credit, they laid claim to humanistic beliefs by which healing came exclusively from inner resources without divine intervention. Although I didn't realize it at the time, I became engaged in the process of integrating my Christian faith with human learning. As my final paper for the summer program, I wrote a critique labeling "non-directive" therapy as a technique for clinical pastoral care, but a theologically deficient theory counter to Christian theology.

When I returned to the seminary in the fall I had little chance to explain why I had learned greater respect for different theological traditions or share my insight into the integration of Christian theology with psychological theory. Another round of conferences was scheduled to see if I had been theologically tainted. When I wrote a paper applying my experience to Romans 5 under the title, "The Neurosis of the Law," the door to the woodshed opened again and I was thoroughly spanked. The very next semester my scholarship was canceled, ostensibly because I had changed my plans about going directly to parish ministry, but not without some evidence of being tainted. Thirty years later, when I returned as President of Asbury Theological Seminary, I had a sharp needle in a humorous story about a canceled scholarship. Even though I was tempted, I held my tongue.

ROWDY AWAKENING

Go forward with me six years after starting my career at Spring Arbor Junior College. I had completed the PhD and started teaching courses in the administration of higher education at the University of Michigan on its Dearborn, Flint, and Grand Rapids campuses. The experience whetted my appetite to beard the lion in the den of the public university. Guided by Dr. Algo Henderson, my mentor, an opportunity for starting a Center for the Study of Higher Education at the Ohio State University opened up. In the interviews for the position, I encountered the most liberal of thinking in educational philosophy. George Marsden, in his book, *The Outrageous Idea of Christian Scholarship*, captures the intellectual reputation for Ohio State by quoting a professor of philosophy:

> Any personal beliefs—religious or otherwise—that are discussed in the classroom have be supported by evidence, and that evidence should meet the standards of the profession. But faith is, by definition, a belief in that for which there is no proof: once a belief can be supported by independent scientific evidence, it loses it religious nature . . . when considering any theory, "the evidence has to carry the day, not the fact that it is Christian."[7]

The School of Education and Psychology had the reputation for being the hotbed for this attitude. Its prided itself in the heritage of Boyd H. Bode, philosophical father of progressive education and passionate pragmatist, who claimed that human experience alone was sufficient to answer the questions of truth and morality. When I researched the history of Dr. Bode, I discovered a path that began as an idealistic young man studying for the ministry before becoming a disciple of John Dewey and William James and then refuting them in favor of radical pragmatism as his own faith position. Boyd Bode personified all of the fears of tainting that made the Christian

7. George Marsden, *The Outrageous Idea of Christian Scholarship*, 25.

colleges so defensive. I can still see the large portrait of Bode at the entrance to the School of Education and still feel the pervasive influence of his thinking in every program. For me to move from Spring Arbor Junior College to The Ohio State University meant riding a pendulum swinging wildly from one philosophical extreme to another.

True to its democratic claims, every candidate for a professorial position at Ohio State had to appear before the whole faculty in a free-for-all over educational philosophy and practice. I sat alone at the front of a large room facing my potential peers. The Dean of the College introduced me and then invited the first question. From the right hand corner came a contentious voice, "What is a theist like you doing in a place like this?" Before I could frame my answer, another voice rang out from the other side of the room, "Why not? Don't we believe in academic freedom?" Almost with one voice, shouts of "Hear, hear!" echoed through the room. The question was answered for me. Even the philosopher who worshiped at the feet of Bode became my stalwart friend. I was set free to teach as I chose without any challenge to my theism.

After the faculty meeting, I accepted the position as Assistant Professor and Director of the Center for the Study of Higher Education. Although God had clearly guided my life to that moment, I expect that my aspirations to test the waters of a public university probably motivated the move. Leaving the security of position and family at Spring Arbor Junior College, we sold our home and moved to an apartment in Upper Arlington, Ohio with two children and a third to be born in November, 1960. God's grace has a lot of latitude because one year at Ohio State let me stretch my wings, soar toward the sun without getting singed, and see the affirming vision for a future in Christian higher education. I would never be defensive again. Nor would I ever stop searching for the common cause that would bring us together.

5

Teachable Moment

A TEACHABLE MOMENT AWAITS future leaders of evangelical Christian colleges in the history of American higher education. That moment came for me at the Ohio State University when I taught graduate classes in the history, philosophy, and curriculum of American higher education. While I had read the standard works of authors in the field, I had not yet seen how their stories converge with sharp distinction between the secular university and the Christian college. The defection of colonial Christian colleges from their original faith position drew my attention. Although the story has been written time and time again under the euphemism of "the slippery slope,"[1] it reads differently to a person who has been inside the evangelical Christian college, but then transfers to a national research university as a professor in the field of higher education. In this role, I learned the meaning of the proverb, "Iron sharpens iron" (Prov 27:17).

THROUGH THE LENS OF HISTORY

The first lesson for a student of American higher education is to learn that our leading institutions of today were founded on biblically-based, Christ-centered convictions. How many times have we read that Harvard was founded with the chief aim that "Every one shall consider the Mayne End

1. Burtchaell, *The Dying of the Light*, 837.

of his life and studies, to know God and Jesus Christ, which is Eternall life"?[2] Who can doubt the sweeping influence of the Great Awakening over Yale when New Light repentance and conversion set the tone for the campus? How can we forget that Eleazer Wheelock, a Congregational minister, founding Dartmouth College for the purpose of evangelizing Indian tribes?

What happened? Historians offer varying theories, usually grounded in cultural drifts away from Christian roots and highlighted by intellectual shifts from revelation to reason. Most often, the reasons for the defection of Christian colleges are stated in negative terms, citing the board, president, faculty, and denominational leadership for failing to keep the faith. Rather than repeating these negative theories, let me advance to a positive view for sustaining the academic and spiritual integrity of the Christian college based upon the same history.

First and foremost, *the integrity of the Christian college is sustained by a mission statement that binds Christian faith together with policy, planning, and practice.* Mission statements of colonial Christian colleges do not meet this criterion. Harvard, as we have already noted, was founded with the expectation that students would "consider the Mayne end of life and studies, to know God and Jesus Christ, which is Eternall life." Periodic revival among the students seemed to be the holding power for the mission. Meanwhile, slippage of purpose in board planning, presidential leadership, faculty commitments, curriculum offerings, and church connections undermined these moments of spiritual recovery. Without common agreement on a centering truth that encompassed the concept, curriculum, and climate of the campus, erosion of the original mission was all but inevitable. Christian colleges were doomed to defection because they submitted themselves to the whims of a changing culture while holding on to pietistic hope. Colonial Christian colleges needed a mission statement that was a guide for change rather an object of change.

Second, *the integrity of the Christian college is sustained by a board of governors or trustees who understand that their primary purpose is to preserve and advance the mission of the institution.* Boards of all colleges and universities tend to migrate toward zones of caution or comfort where they feel most at home.

In colonial times, clergy dominated the boards and put priority upon theological and behavioral concerns consistent with the disciplines of their

2. Brubacher and Rudy, *Higher Education in Transition,* 8.

denomination. At the same time, they were least comfortable in such areas as faculty instruction and curriculum development.

Skewed policies resulted. Board agendas focused attention on spiritual issues with board members using the leverage of church funding to assure their power base. Other issues, such instruction and curriculum, were dumped into the same bucket. Policies and practices followed the same course. As long as faculty members, especially those in theology, met the artificial test of orthodoxy, all hands were off.

In areas of theology or morality, the clergy-dominated board micromanaged; but in the areas of instruction and curriculum, it turned matters over to the president and stepped in only if a crisis ensued. Like the human body that marshals its defenses to fight one disease, another part is left exposed.

A pointed lesson about board governance comes out of this review. One is the importance of board composition and the power of diversity in representation, not just in gender and race, but in vocation and interest.

This lesson applies to contemporary as well as colonial college boards. The heavy shift from clergy to laity, emphasizing work, wealth, and wisdom, may change the focus of the board but not the evidence of migration toward a zone of caution or comfort. With the weight of board membership tipped toward the business community, we can expect their expertise and interest to move toward finance, especially budgets and endowments. For Christian college boards to fulfill their primary purpose of preserving and advancing the mission of the institution, there is no substitute for the checks and balance of professional and personal diversity.

Third, *the integrity of a Christian college is sustained by a presidential leader who sees the vision, states the mission, and sets its tone for whole campus.* Just as the Alpine peaks rise high out of a cloudy landscape and stand tall against a clear blue sky, the history of Christian colleges in American higher education can be written in the stature and significance of its presidents.

At the height of their influence, an overwhelming majority of Christian college presidents was clergy. With the complementary strengths of church support, clergy boards, and clergy faculty in the field of theology, they enjoyed the leadership leverage to hold the college on its course, change its direction, or renew its spirit.

Timothy Dwight, president of Yale, and grandson of Jonathan Edwards, is an example. Prior to Dwight's arrival as president in 1795, Yale had the notorious reputation as a hotbed of heresy with a moral climate in the residence halls described as "the secret nurseries of every vice and the cages of unclean birds."[3]

After assuming office, President Dwight used his inaugural sermon to invite all of the students to an open forum on the Christian faith. Then, in a president's chapel series, he preached the Word with such anointing that more than half of the Yale student body came to Christ before the end of the year. Timothy Dwight leaves us with the indelible message that the president of the Christian college has moral and spiritual leverage to set the tone for the campus as well as see its vision and model its mission.

Fifth, *the integrity of the Christian college is sustained by a faculty of persons thoroughly committed to Jesus Christ, knowledgeable as scholars in their disciplines, dedicated as students of scripture, sensitive to the mind of the Spirit, and called to the integration of faith and learning in their research, teaching, and service.* A sobering fact out of the history of the Christian college in American higher education confronts us: The faculty has the power to confirm or cancel the vision, mission, policies, and practices of the board and its president. Because faculty members serve at the intersection of the classroom where their minds and spirits personally influence students, they are at the pivot point for the Christian college. Issues of theological position, philosophical thought, and cultural change become their responsibility to interpret and resolve. In the early years of the colonial Christian college, the theological battles between Calvinists and Arminians or between Old and New Lights ultimately became their warfare. Later, when Enlightenment philosophy pitted human reason against divine revelation, the faculty determined the direction of the institution, even when official pronouncements remained unchanged. On and on, through the challenges of empiricism, fundamentalism, and liberalism, the history of change, and often defection, in the Christian college can be written through personalized flow of faculty influence. Not even the temporary renewal of spiritual revival among students could counter the power of the faculty in giving the Christian college its text and tone. As the faculty goes, the institution goes.

Critics are quick to blame the faculty for the defection of Christian colleges from the faith. To be sure, they have their share of the blame, but boards and presidents may be equally or more guilty of a false assumption. Christian colleges recruit faculty members who are personally committed Christians and professionally prepared scholars. It is assumed that the

3. Ibid., 41.

integration of faith and learning is automatic. It is not. Graduate studies in a given field go narrow and deep, but not broad and across disciplines. Little opportunity is given for reflection on integrative questions between faith and learning.

It cannot be assumed that Christian scholars are students of the Word. They may or not be. Yet, the integration of faith and learning requires sufficient grounding in both revelation and reason in order to ask the critical questions and come to sound conclusions. Here is where boards and presidents exercise leadership. If faculty is a priority for their leadership, they will not only hire committed Christians and qualified scholars for positions, but also provide resources for an intentional program of faculty development that builds upon their motivation to serve as Christian scholars, orients them to the theological convictions and philosophical assumptions underlying Christian higher education, creates a format for addressing the issues of integration, and provides senior mentors to guide them in their growth. The esteem of the Christian scholar will rise because teaching the integration of faith and learning is a distinctive task that contributes to the church as well as the academy.

Sixth, *the integrity of the Christian college is sustained by a general education curriculum in the Christian liberal arts that serves as a solid center to balance out the shifting of professional studies.* The integration of faith and learning is not exclusive to the Christian college. Any general education curriculum that is the required core for the student learning experience has to have an anchor point of faith around which the courses are organized. As we have already noted, Harvard College was founded under the faith position of "Veritas." Consequently, the strength of its general education curriculum in classical studies set the pace for years to come. When "Veritas" was downgraded to "veritas," however, its program in general education lost its organizing center and opened the door to a curriculum later described as a "cafeteria" with multiple options for every taste. Harvard has been scrambling for a curriculum in general education ever since. Brubacher and Rudy, in their book, *Higher Education in Transition: A History of American Colleges and Universities,* sum up the futile search when they write,

> The history of the curriculum, thus, had taken the form of a vast
> Hegelian triad wherein the thesis of the early nineteenth century
> had been prescription, the antithesis in the later nineteenth century

had been election, and the synthesis of the twentieth century had been concentration and distribution . . . Hence the kind of synoptic integration characteristic of liberal education went by default.[4]

Even Harvard's celebrated volume, *General Education in a Free Society* (1945), failed to coordinate the curriculum or integrate instruction around a primary principle. Like Whitman's "noiseless, patient spider," the Harvard faculty cast out filament after filament, hoping that one would catch and hold. William James' "pragmatism," John Dewey's "instrumentalism," and Thorndike's "behaviorism" all failed to rally the faculty as their article of faith. Instead, as Talcott Parsons argues in his book, *The American University,* general education at Harvard suffered separation of the "cognitive complex" (science) from the "moral evaluative complex" (humanities) under the influence of Presidents James Conant and Derek Bok.[5] Robert Bellah picks up this thought and concludes, "Without the integrative context that classical American philosophy might have provided, they have only become more disparate ever since."[6]

Students are the losers. Bellah quotes from the commencement oration of a Harvard graduate who reflected on his education, "They tell us that it is heresy to suggest the superiority of some value, fantasy to believe in a moral argument, slavery to submit to a judgment sounder than our own. The freedom of the day is the freedom to devote ourselves to any values we please, on the mere condition that we do not believe them to be true."[7]

A PLACE TO STAND

Through the lens of history, then, we see the potential for the Christian college to make its distinctive mark on American higher education. Secular higher education searches for what we have. With the firm biblical conviction that all things come together in Christ, an integrative experience in the Christian liberal arts is the purpose to which we are called. No self-pity because we cannot compete with the reputation and resources of elitist colleges and research universities. If we are true to our mission in curriculum and instruction, we serve in the superlative.

4. Ibid., 217.
5. Bellah, *The Good Society,* 166.
6. Ibid.
7. Ibid., 4.

One year and two summers on the faculty of the Ohio State University brought these insights together for me. Along the way, my primary assignment was to develop a Center for the Study of Higher Education. The proposal was presented and approved by the faculty of the School of Education and Psychology in the early spring of 1961. A few days later, the Dean of the School called me into his office. Blowing smoke rings from his pipe, he said, "David, I have bad news for you. The Ohio legislature has declared a moratorium on all new programs in the University. If you are to see the Center developed, it'll take time and you will have to give your life to it." I walked out disheartened, but only for a short time. When Dr. Algo Henderson heard about the decision, he called to invite me to come back to the University of Michigan as Assistant Director at the Center from which I had graduated. His offer was accepted immediately and we began to hunt for a home in Ann Arbor in anticipation of the move in time for the opening of the fall semester. Nothing opened up and we wondered why. Then, the couple to whom we had sold our home in Spring Arbor defaulted on the sale and walked away. It appeared as if we would have to move back to Spring Arbor while I commuted 56 miles back and forth to Ann Arbor.

God showed his hand when Hugh A. White, Chair of the Board of Trustees at Spring Arbor Junior College called and invited me to the presidency with the challenge of developing a new, four-year Christian liberal arts college. His invitation, however, compounded our dilemma. We had signed a contract with the University of Michigan and made a personal pledge to Dr. Henderson. Our prayers took on intensity as we puzzled over the timing for the two invitations. Finally, the decision settled into the question, "Do we want to lead in the field of higher education or at an institution of Christian higher education?" Both areas held high interest, but the deciding factor had to be the call of God. With great trepidation, we determined to meet Dr. Henderson, share our conflict, and let his response be our guide. If he asked me to honor the contract, I would do it.

Our whole family, including Jan's parents, traveled to Ann Arbor, ate lunch at Bill Knapp's Restaurant and then sat on the grass waiting for me at the intersection where one road went east to the University of Michigan and the other went west toward Spring Arbor Junior College. Dr Henderson listened to my full story, including my commitment to the contract. After I finished he followed his usual pattern of twisting and untwisting a paper clip before responding. Then, my esteemed mentor and avowed agnostic said, "David, I know where your heart is. The main purpose of the

Center is to prepare college presidents and, if you choose the presidency at Spring Arbor, we will be proud of you."

I was set free. All of the shackles of doubt fell off and I knew where God was calling me. The moment still registers as one of the most liberating moments of my life. Like Cyrus of old, Algo Henderson proved to be a servant of God. My debt to him can never be repaid because years later I learned that our meeting came just after he had been informed that his wife had terminal cancer. He counted on me helping with the directorship during his wife's illness and then assuming responsibility for the Center so that he could take a long-deferred sabbatical. My freedom came at his sacrifice. Thanks to him, I became the youngest college president in the nation at the time, with the formidable task of bringing my insights from the history of American higher education into the experimental start-up of a four-year Christian liberal arts college.

6

Formative Era

AMERICAN HIGHER EDUCATION HIGH-STEPPED into the 1960s. The optimism of democratic faith never burned brighter as the system of higher education expanded along with public confidence. Added support came from the alliance of higher education with the power of the military-industrial complex, the surge in religious interest, the vision of youthful leadership in political office, the promise of urban renewal, the quietude of racial conflict, and the challenge of the race to the moon. College campuses were calm, so calm in fact, that one observer said, "The minds of students are as quiet as mice." Symbolic of the era, the Ford Foundation touted ten-year, long-range planning for institutions of higher education. Generous grants were given and everyone followed the Pied Piper with glossy brochures projecting idealistic goals for the decade.

A RAINBOW GONE TO SMASH

But, as Bob Dylan sang so prophetically, something was "Blowin' in the Wind." Before the decade was over, the democratic dream turned into a nightmare, political idealism would be in shambles, urban areas would be wastelands, religious interest would be dulled, civil rights would be contested in violence, and traditional moral values would be sullied. Again, the campus became the sensor for the revolution. Student minds awakened with anger, condemned established authority, and trashed the offices of their presidents. Indicative of the happenings, ten-year plans of colleges and universities disappeared from public view and began gathering dust on the shelf. Like the little boy who was fascinated at the shimmering colors of an oil slick on the road, our society as well as our system of higher education looked like "a rainbow gone to smash."

Most Christian colleges sat on the sidelines during the violence of these eruptions. From the grandstand, we embraced Kennedy's dream, grieved at his death, sympathized with the marchers at Selma, tended to buy into the domino theory in terms of Vietnam, doubted the Great Society, condemned the revelers at Woodstock, commended our students for refusing to be a part of violent protest, and joined the movement of relational theology to prove that we were O.K. At the same time, small, unaccredited Christian colleges got a new lease on life. Just as the G.I. Bill had provided a financial lifeline for small colleges in the 1950s, the passage of the Higher Education Act of 1965 opened the door of opportunity for students in both public and private institutions. Even unaccredited Christian colleges could participate in the program with three letters from accredited schools who would accept their students for transfer.

RED FLAGS FLY

Despite these gains, the hammer of doubt pounded down on the future of small Christian colleges. In 1961, Earl J. McGrath, future Commissioner of Higher Education for the United States, wrote an article entitled "The Future of the Church-related College." Having witnessed the dilution of the Christian faith and the decline of the liberal arts curriculum, he posted the dire warning:

> All those who view these institutions with a deceiving sentimentalism and nostalgia must conclude that in the absence of a rededication to undergraduate liberal arts education within the Christian tradition, the Protestant college as such is as near to extinction as the whooping crane.[1]

Colleges that wanted to address McGrath's concern, however, were plagued by rising financial deficits. At the end of the decade, William Jellema, in a study of 554 private colleges sponsored by the American Association of Colleges and published in 1971 under the title, *From Red to Black?*:

1. McGrath, "The Future of the Church-related College," 45.

Special Preliminary Report on the Financial Status, Present and Projected, of Private Institutions of Higher Learning, revealed dire statistics about their present and future financial condition. At the heart of issue was the deficit between rising tuition costs and institutionally funded student aid. A follow-up study a year later showed that the gap had widened by 25 percent in one year and threatened to spiral out of control. Without the infusion of substantial resources for student financial aid, Jellema predicted that only a few private colleges would be in his sample a decade later.

MENTORS FOR A ROOKIE

At the same time, resonant voices of Christian scholars were coming through loud and clear. Only when I look back at the 1960s when I was a fledging Christian college president do I realize the formative impact that key Christian leaders had on my life and thought. Long before the idea of mentoring became popular in leadership development, I had the benefit of learning from of the greatest Christian minds of the twentieth century.

Arthur Holmes, Professor of Philosophy at Wheaton College, was the first lecturer we invited to speak on the subject of integrating faith and learning at Spring Arbor College. Professor Holmes drew everyone to rapt attention with his opening question, "Then why a Christian college?" Time and again, he repeated his foundational premise that "All truth is God's truth." He answered his own question that day and later in his book, *The Idea of a Christian College,* when he said, "Its distinctive should be an education that cultivates the creative and active integration of faith and learning, of faith and culture."[2]

Frank Gaebelein joined the company of the best of Christian thinkers with his concept of Christ-centered education as headmaster of Stony Brook Academy. The memory of my meeting with him at the Cosmos Club in Washington, DC is forever etched in my memory. Frank likened Christian higher education to a stake and a tether. He said that the firmness of the stake in commitment to Jesus Christ determined the length of tether in the search for truth. If the stake was firm, the tether could play out into risky issues of faith and learning, but if the stake was shaky, a lengthy tether can come loose from the stake and become an end in itself, flying wildly without a center. The lesson has stayed with me for a lifetime.

2. Holmes, *The Idea of a Christian College,* 6

Elton Trueblood, the Quaker philosopher, stood tall among leading Christian thinkers in the 1960s. While avoiding the theological controversies among liberals, fundamentalists, and evangelicals, he lifted the meaning of Christian faith to its highest levels by sound reasoning, passionate commitment, and selfless service. Trueblood spoke at the 1967 commencement of Spring Arbor College. As he stepped to the rostrum, he pulled from his pocket the crumpled page of a yellow legal pad, spread it out before him, and began to speak from the scribbled notes that were visible from my position behind him. At first, I felt incensed by the thought that he had not adequately prepared for such an important occasion in the life of our college and our students. But, true to form, Trueblood had rapt attention from all his hearers as he defined intellectual integrity for the Christian as rigorous faith, rigorous thought, and rigorous spiritual discipline. His closing words could be etched in stone, "It is the vocation of Christians in every generation to outthink all opposition." Three years later, Trueblood's yellowed notes matured in his book, *The New Man for Our Time*, with the same unforgettable words concluding his writing.[3]

Bernard Ramm, the Baptist theologian, is remembered as one of the evangelical Christianity's leading thinkers in the 1960s. Even though Carl Henry suspected Ramm's acceptance of Karl Barth, their names are often mentioned together. Shortly after Professor Ramm wrote his book, *The Christian College in the Twentieth Century*, he and I shared the platform at a conference of Christian higher education at Olivet Nazarene College. Although I was scheduled to speak, I became an eager learner at Ramm's feet. As we talked about the meaning of integration in Christian higher education, he laid out three options for the teaching-learning process.

First, when the Christian scholar is exploring the interaction between revelation and reason, the result may be *concurrence* between the two ways of knowing truth. For instance, although revelation and reason may differ on how life began, they agree that human beings are rational, thinking and acting creatures distinct from other animals.

Second, in the search for truth, revelation and reason may come into *conflict*. Referring again to human beings, revelation tells us that we are inherently sinful while reason may conclude that we are inherently good. In such a case, faith must reject reason because of the final authority of revealed truth.

3. Trueblood, *The New Man for Our Time*, 26.

Third, because neither revelation nor reason gives us all of the answers, the integrative quest may bring us to *imponderables* for which we have to say with humility, "We do not know." Again, with regard to human nature, there are mysteries of biogenetics, neuroscience, human motivation, and even moral or spiritual impulses that continue to confound us. Rather than closing the gap by biased assumptions, the Christian scholar becomes a colleague with other scholars for research in the field of the imponderables. Bernard Ramm's insights decisively influenced our method of instruction in Christian higher education.

Carl F. H. Henry, as editor of *Christianity Today*, held center stage among Christian scholars because he could speak from the bully pulpit of a magazine with a circulation of more than 100,000 readers. Even though Carl led the charge for Calvinist theology and had doubts about the academic credibility of Wesleyans because of our allegedly "soft view" on the inerrancy of scripture, I invited him to be a participant on an a scholarly panel at my inauguration as President of Spring Arbor College in 1963. He graciously accepted and joined the company of Lewis Mayhew, a leading voice for the liberal arts college, but self-proclaimed secular humanist, and Morris Keeton, father of experimental education and adult learning. Carl led the way by laying out the tenets of the classical curriculum and rebuking any muddle-headed thinking that failed to meet his expectations for the Christian liberal arts. His partners on the panel took the bait and fired back. The liveliest of debates followed, but not with rancor. At the end of the day, the protagonists shook hands and headed for the coffee shop to continue their conversation. Out of that event, the tone was set for a campus climate open for the discussion of delicate issues and differing viewpoints because we followed Frank Gaebelein's model and drove deeply the stake of our commitment in the person of Jesus Christ. Carl Henry remained an edgy friend for life who never failed to challenge me, whether writing articles for *Christianity Today*, speaking at the National Association of Evangelicals, or strategizing about the future of Christian higher education.

Ernest Boyer, future U.S. Commissioner of Education, Chancellor of the New York State University System, and President of the Carnegie Foundation, began his career as Academic Dean at Upland College in California. Our paths crossed at a Council for the Advancement of Small Colleges conference at Westmont College in 1963. Both of us had a special interest in the integration of faith and learning, especially as it related to moral questions rising out of a changing culture that created controversy and frequently divided Christian believers. A year after our first meeting, Ernie received a sizeable grant from the Ford Foundation to experiment with the academic calendar at Upland College and address the divisive issue of nuclear warfare on a campus with a historical background in pacifism. He invited me to come as his guest to observe and advise on the experiment. Ernie proposed what was later known as the 4-1-4 academic calendar, with four courses in the fall and spring semesters interspersed by the month of January when the whole campus concentrated on one subject. Risking the wrath of constituents, especially pacifists in the community, Ernie brought internationally known speakers from different sides of the issue to the campus and engaged them in brisk, but not hostile, dialogue. Then, out of the mix, he raised the question about the integration of Christian faith as a way of understanding and responding to the issue. Nothing was settled at the moment, but it was clear that the Upland campus had a glimpse of what it means to be a "learning community." Ernest Boyer dared to do what I dreamed of doing in Christian higher education.

Senator Mark Hatfield accepted our invitation to speak at the Spring Arbor College Commencement in 1966. He had the reputation as a conservative Christian with progressive politics whose integrity kept him in trouble with extremists on both sides of the theological spectrum. His commencement address paved the way for us to understand the title of his future book, *Between a Rock and a Hard Place*, when he applied his mantra for a Christian in politics. The senator told our graduates, "You can compromise on timing, wording and procedure, but never on principle."

A decade later, on a flight from Washington DC to Seattle, my seat partner was a lobbyist for a major industry in the State of Oregon. I had been approached about running for Congress from the State of Washington, so I asked him, "Would you recommend a career in politics for a young man like me?" His eyes narrowed and the tone of his voice left no doubt, "Never. I have seen young idealists like you come to Washington and be corrupted within six months." I swallowed hard, but dared to ask, "What about Mark Hatfield?" His face brightened with his answer, "Oh, he's different." The senator's reputation for integrity in a corrupting climate more than confirmed his working principle that applies, not just in politics, but in any leadership position to which a Christian is called.

Charles Malik, President of the United Nations, followed Mark Hatfield as our commencement speaker in 1967. His outspoken Christian testimony drew us to travel to the American University in Lebanon and invite him to our campus. Perhaps our youthful enthusiasm coupled with the ability to articulate our commitment to intellectual integrity and spiritual passion won the day. Dr. Malik accepted our invitation and arrived on campus the day of the outbreak of the Six Day War between Israel and Syria. Communications with Lebanon had been cut off so Malik did not know the status of his nation in the conflict or whether or not his family was safe. As he spoke to our graduates, an aide stood in the wings with a radio and a phone ready to bring word to Dr. Malik. The crisis setting, however, did not dull the keen edge of truth that our speaker personified in his life and work. As he also wrote later in his monograph, *The Two Tasks*, he pressed home the point, "Responsible Christians face two tasks, that of saving the soul and that of saving the mind."[4] Charles Malik joined my hall of heroes calling for the integration of faith and learning in Christian higher education.

When I am asked what I would change in my educational career, I answer, "Before becoming a college president, I wish that I have served as an apprentice to a great Christian leader." Now, in looking back, I see that God gave me more than that kind of experience through the mentors I have named. Arthur Holmes, Frank Gaebelein, Carl Henry, Bernard Ramm, Ernest Boyer, Elton Trueblood, Mark Hatfield, Charles Malik—who could ask for greater minds and souls as mentors for a young president?

UNEXPECTED INVITATION

Shortly after assuming the presidency of Spring Arbor College in 1961, I was surprised by a phone call from Novice Fawcett, President of the Ohio State University, for whom I had done the research and wrote the report on the trimester calendar as an option to the quarter system at the university. Even though our personal contact was limited during my year at Ohio State, he was now calling to ask me to consider the position as the first president of the newly-developed Wright State University in Dayton, Ohio. Because Ohio State University controlled the state's system of higher education and President Fawcett stood at the top, I knew that he was talking about an appointment, not a search process. His voice grew in excitement as he explained the opportunity to lead in bringing a new state university into being. But the same voice slumped in disbelief when I thanked him and then said, "No. I feel called of God to the presidency of Spring Arbor College." Taken back by my response, President Fawcett asked, "How much

4. Malik, *The Two Tasks*, 34

are you making?" I heard a whoosh of bewilderment` when I answered, "$10,000." Excitement rushed back into his voice, "$10,000? Dave, I'm talking about $25,000 to start and its onward and upward from there!" Instead of pausing to consider the temptation, I repeated my commitment to the call of God and our talk ended on a note of disbelief. President Fawcett's invitation goes down in my personal history as one of the "roads not taken." God confirmed his calling and my decision in the mentors who shaped my thinking and challenged my commitment to the integration of Christian faith and human learning.

7

Testing Ground

IF YOU WANT TO change the curriculum in higher education, start a college. Otherwise, the old adage holds true, "It takes at least ten years for a new idea to get from the drawing board into the curriculum of a college." The history of American higher education bears this out. Courageous college presidents throughout history have proposed grand designs for an experimental curriculum in general education integrated around their particular ideal for liberal learning. Two of these experiments stand out as models for studying curriculum theories in American higher education.

THE GREAT BOOKS CURRICULUM

President Robert Maynard Hutchins, dubbed the "Boy Wonder" at the University of Chicago because of his youth, is best known for his plan to recreate the undergraduate curriculum around "Great Books of the Western World" in the classical tradition. For students of the history of higher education, Hutchins' plan is introduced as the ultimate model for an integrated curriculum in the liberal arts. With freeing of the mind for critical thinking as his mantra, Hutchins jettisoned all existing courses and proposed a required, comprehensive undergraduate curriculum in the Great Books of Western civilization. Ranging from the Bible to the classics of ancient Greece, students at each undergraduate level read one book at a time as the basis for class discussion, debate, and discovery of lasting values. With evangelistic fervor, Hutchins introduced his plan in 1952, "This is more than a set of books and more than a liberal education. *Great Books of the Western World* is an act of piety. Here are the sources of our being. Here is our heritage. This is the West. This is its meaning for mankind."[1]

As intriguing as it was to the scholarly mind, Hutchins failed to win the faculty with his radical idealism. Angry at the academy, he left Chicago to pursue his own path at the Center for Democratic Studies in Santa Barbara, California. Hutchins' legacy continues at St. John's College, in Santa Fe, New Mexico and Annapolis, Maryland, where the Great Books curriculum defines its character and its curriculum. Hutchins' grand idea ultimately had minimal impact on the curriculum landscape of American higher education.

THE ANTIOCH PLAN

Algo Henderson championed another attempt at an integrative curriculum when he was President of Antioch College, Ohio. Building upon his commitment to democratic freedom in higher education as proposed by the Truman Commission, he integrated his ideal into an innovative curriculum giving credit for academic study, work programs, and community participation. Henderson attracted bright and independent students who fit the curriculum. Antioch became a brand for its off-beat students who labored and learned while majoring in social activism. Like so many grand designs, the Antioch Plan attracted national attention and praise from scholars, but ran aground under the economic pressures when student interest returned to more traditional studies and professional interests. Years after Algo Henderson's time, Antioch bottomed out in resources and, in order to survive, joined the ranks of colleges specializing in offering adult degree completion programs in multiple cities throughout the nation.

THE QUESTION OF SUSTAINABILITY

The lack of sustainability in Hutchins' and Henderson's ventures raises the question, "Why?"

Frank Gaebelein's analogy of the stake and the tether comes back as a lesson for all of higher education. Sustainability in a curriculum depends

1. Hutchins, "*The Great Books of the Western World*, History."

upon a deeply-driven stake in a standard of truth that interprets human history, judges right and wrong, and casts a vision for the future. Unless all members of the academic community are personally committed to that standard of truth, the tether of learning flies out all over the educational landscape. When this happens, a general education in the liberal arts is crowded out by two threats. Internally, there is the threat of proliferation in new courses, majors, degrees, and new delivery systems. As traditional disciplines of learning expand and new disciplines come on line, faculty will want to add courses in order to keep pace with their field. Boards, presidents, and academic deans are not far behind, proposing new fields with academic prestige, market value, and financial return.

Add the external threat of certification for professional programs, such as nursing, business, and computer technology. As professional requirements increase and begin in the freshman and sophomore years, it is the liberal arts that suffer. With accreditation determined by the profession, the liberal arts college has no choice if the program is to be offered and the students are to be certified. Professional accreditation is often the culprit. Whenever our faculties sought national accreditation for a professional field, such as education, nursing, business, and engineering, recommendations for added courses intruding on general education were the outcome. Slowly, but surely, general education becomes a hodge-podge of elective and distributive courses in the well-known "cafeteria" curriculum. To reverse the process is notoriously slow and often defeated. We know why it is easier to start a college than to change a curriculum.

EXPERIMENTAL STARTUP

As the new President of Spring Arbor Junior College in 1961, a clear mandate was handed to me by the Board of Trustees, with concurrence of the faculty. My task was to develop a fully-accredited, four-year Christian liberal arts college at Spring Arbor. All of my formal experience in higher education came into focus and every lesson I had ever learned would be put to the test. Even though my undergraduate and graduate studies resembled a crab walk meandering between history and theology, theology and psychology, psychology and higher education, God knew what he was doing and where he wanted to take me. My first task was to gather what I had learned and translate it into a viable plan for starting and sustaining a new Christian liberal arts college at Spring Arbor.

As the starting point, our board, administration and faculty determined that the integration of Christian faith and human learning would be the lodestar by which we would navigate through the uncertain waters of planning and implementing a new Christian liberal arts college. Undoubtedly, we would make mistakes and have to make adjustments, but with that integrative principle driving every facet of institutional development, we were confident of the start-up. Sustainability, however, would prove to be the acid test. Could we achieve what Hutchins and Henderson had failed to do? While only time could judge our longevity and effectiveness, we counted upon our roots in the idea of integrating Christian faith and human learning to make a difference. What then were the start-up stages of development aimed at sustainability?

ANCHOR POINTS

First, we established an integrative center. Without the slightest hesitation, we drove our stake deeply into the person of Jesus Christ as the perspective for learning. Later, in faculty debate, some would question whether we should substitute an "a" for "the" in setting the stake. Could a liberal arts college dedicated to "freeing the mind" and "searching for truth" be unequivocally committed to a single perspective for learning without submitting to the arrogance of a fundamentalism that denies or demeans any other perspective? Does academic freedom mean that all perspectives of truth are equal? Can a scholar claim to be completely objective?

Huston Smith, in his book, *The Purposes of Higher Education*, dared to call out hidden prejudices in academic scholarship. He wrote,

> Only by becoming aware not only of what it consciously intends but also of what it unconsciously assumes can education adequately define its aims and clarify its methods. As long as it ignores its value presuppositions, its teaching will be secretly divided against itself in its unconscious depths. Such education will be inevitably enervated by this hidden conflict, and display unmistakable neurotic symptoms in its overt program.[2]

George Marsden reinforced the same thought when he wrote, "The convention of insisting that all scholars and teachers pose as disinterested observers is more misleading than a general rule of frank identification of one's

2. Smith, *The Purposes of Higher Education*, 6.

biases." Christians who take the Word of God as their final authority and agree that "All things come together in Christ" are honest scholars. Centered in that confidence there is every reason to explore alternative ways of knowing truth without nursing a hidden prejudice.

Second, we articulated an integrative concept. Building upon our center stake in the person of Jesus Christ, we went deeply in the Word of God to explore the implications of the cardinal doctrines of creation, redemption and sanctification for integration with the Christian liberal arts.[3] In creation, we saw the potential for scholarship; in redemption, the promise of sonship; and in sanctification, the possibility of servanthood.

From there we advanced to recognition that the incarnation, crucifixion and resurrection of Jesus Christ revealed a worldview that could be infused into the curriculum, taught in the classroom, and modeled in the campus community, and enacted in the contemporary world. When all of these pieces came together, we framed the Spring Arbor Concept as the mission statement for all further institutional development:

> Spring Arbor College is a community of learners engaged in the
> serious study of the liberal arts, personally committed to Jesus
> Christ as the perspective for learning, and pledged to critical par-
> ticipation in the contemporary world.[4]

With an eye on our target audience of junior and senior high school students, graphic symbols representing each aspect of the Concept were embedded in a logo that would be at the forefront of all future communication from the College—a lighted lamp of learning ("serious study"), intersected by the cross of Jesus Christ ("personal commitment") whose arms reached out ("critical participation") to embrace the global ellipse of the contemporary world. Almost sixty years after its inauguration, the Spring Arbor Concept and its unmistakable logo are still essentially intact. Accrediting teams never fail to commend the College for a mission statement that students know and can explain.

Third, we designed an integrative curriculum. Faculty engagement rode high at each stage of development for the new college. After thoroughly absorbing select books related to issues of integrating faith and learning, including the report of the faculty study committee at St. Olaf College[5] and

3. The detailed study of our search is found in Beebe and Kulaga, *Concept for a College* and my *Megatruth: Hi-truth for a Hi-tech World*.

4. Beebe and Kulaga, *Concept for a College*, viii.

5. St. Olaf Self-Study Committee, *Integration in the Christian Liberal Arts College*.

H. Richard Niebuhr's *Christ and Culture*,[6] faculty energy peaked with the challenge of writing an experimental curriculum called the Christian Perspective in the Liberal Arts (CPLA). For the general education courses required of freshmen and sophomores, each liberal arts division accepted the assignment to conceive a course or courses organized around the central idea of the discipline, extended to give a fair hearing to alternative ideas, and advanced through the integrative process that we had learned from Bernard Ramm. In biology, for example, the course title "Cell and System in Living Organisms" told its own story, and in psychology "Mind and Motivation in Human Behavior" opened wide the doors to alternative theories, the integrative process, and the Christian worldview.

In support of these integrative courses, the 4–1–4 academic calendar was adopted with a view to multiple options for the month of January, such as cross-cultural learning, a module on a contemporary issue and, in the sophomore year, an exploratory experience in vocational choice with a Spring Arbor College alumnus in the same field. The CPLA curriculum concluded with a Senior Seminar requiring presentation of a senior paper that took an interdisciplinary and integrative approach to a contemporary issue.

As would be expected, the students going through the curriculum for the first time were baffled by this approach to Christian higher education, but by the time that they defended their senior paper, they often commented, "Now I understand what it is all about." With relevant, but minimal, revisions for changing circumstances, the CPLA curriculum is still the centerpiece for Spring Arbor College (now University).

Fourth, we created an integrative campus climate. Separation between curricular and co-curricular climates is a problem for all institutions of higher education, but for the Christian college it contradicts the claim for holistic learning. As we learned from the history of American higher education, even a spiritual revival can be limited to the co-curricular environment with little impact upon curriculum and instruction. Chapel, of course, is always a conundrum.

When Elton Trueblood visited a Christian college campus, his first question was to ask about the vitality of chapel and its relationship to the academic community. Agreeing with him, our approach was to identify the chapel as "the President's Course" after the pattern of the colonial Christian college. At least three times each semester I spoke on the distinctives of the

6. Niebuhr, *Christ and Culture*.

Christian college with an emphasis upon integration of faith and learning as a complement to the ongoing education in the classroom.

Later on, we adopted Dr. Trueblood's idea of "the Cadre" as a network of small spiritual growth groups organized around subjects of common interest. The intention was to cross-fertilize the natural tendency for students to cluster in specialty groups, such as athletics, music, residence halls, and major fields of study. Scores of other ideas went into the effort to create a campus community in which the curricular and co-curricular flows merged in the integrative purpose. Otherwise, the informal flow of co-curricular attitudes can run cross-wise to the formal flow of the curriculum. Sooner or later, the sustainability of integrity in the Christian college will depend upon the success of their merger.

Fifth, we projected an integrative master plan for campus development. Working on the architect's premise that "We build buildings and then they build us," priorities for future construction followed the same integrative principle. First in line was a new library as the symbolic "mind" at the center of the campus. Our first faculty appointment was a Ph.D. in Library Science who culled the collection of useless volumes and received budget priority to build a highly selective collection that resourced the CPLA curriculum. A student center and dining commons symbolized the "heart" of the campus, featuring a circular, sunken forum in the floor for community discussion of contemporary issues, topical seminars, and organizational meetings.

PLAN FOR THE PAPER COLLEGE

From these five anchor points, a strategic, long-range plan became our blueprint for a self-study that would be submitted to the North Central Association for accreditation as a four-year, Christian liberal arts college.

At the beginning, however, we had to make the unpopular decision to cancel some upper division courses that had already been scheduled. Even more difficult was the phone call telling the professor who had been recruited to teach these courses that we would not proceed with an appointment. Instead, we opted to take the risk of submitting our "paper college" plan to North Central for preliminary accreditation as a four-year college.

We were sailing through uncharted waters. The North Central Association required two graduating classes to assess the effectiveness of learning outcomes before granting regional accreditation. We were asking for recognition based upon quality of planning so that we could recruit students for upper division classes with the assurance that they could graduate from an accredited four-year college.

Our meeting with the Commission of Higher Education of the North Central Association proved to be touch-and-go all the way. The commissioners commended the plan but raised tough questions about the reality of achieving the goals. Our executive team left a draining two-hour session in doubt about the likelihood of our success. As we huddled in the hotel room awaiting the decision, we could only ask, "What will we do now?" Our gloom deepened as we realized that we had put our future into a high-risk venture that now seemed destined to fail.

Inside the Commission chambers, pros and cons of our application were being weighed and the cons were winning until the president of Ball State University came forward to say, "The new library is more than a dream. I know the prospective donor and it will be built." On his word, the scales tipped toward of vote of confidence. The Commission voted to grant our "paper college" preliminary accreditation as a four-year Christian liberal arts college with the condition that our status be reviewed *after* we had graduated two senior classes and studied them for the effectiveness of our learning outcomes.

When the phone rang in our hotel room, I turned to my executive team with the gravity of a judge pronouncing a death sentence and said, "Here it comes." But instead of rejection, I heard the Chair of the Commission give extra dignity to the life-changing words, "Congratulations. You have been granted preliminary accreditation by the North Central Association." I don't remember my response except for a gulp of gratitude, "Thanks. We won't let you down."

As soon as the phone hit its cradle, our hotel room exploded with whoops, hugs, tears, and praise to God. Right away, we called to our wives, then sent the joyous news back to campus. Checking out and speeding home, we were greeted by a celebration fit for winning a national championship. In a small but important way, God affirmed the integration of Christian faith and human learning as the fulcrum upon which we would stand to move the world.

PART 2

Generating Mass

*"A movement is formed when
a commanding truth is embraced
by a critical mass"*

8

Converging Search

THE DECADE OF THE 1960s came in with a bang and went out with a whimper. A generation of young leaders carried our hope. Our youthful president John F. Kennedy would transform the White House into Camelot and young mayors, such as John Lindsay of New York, would lead our nation's cities into shining examples of urban renewal. The moon was within reach, not just for space flight but also for a "shining city on a hill" and for equal opportunity in higher education. Assassinations, riots, and protests, however, shook our moral foundations, challenged our established institutions, and rattled our idealistic hopes for our educational systems. Yet, through the darkness of this dire scene four beacons of light broke through giving promise of rebirth for the movement of Christian higher education.

SHIFT #1: FROM SURVIVAL TO SIGNIFICANCE

By 1960, the Council for the Advancement of Small Colleges had gained sufficient stature to shift its focus from institutional survival to educational significance. A major conference on strategic planning for small colleges was held at Westmont College in the summer of 1963. The program featured educators of national note, such as Earl McGrath, John Dale Russell, and Lewis Mayhew, addressing the special role of small colleges in American higher education and society. In one of the workshop sessions, I presented the model for the Christian Perspective in the Liberal Arts at Spring Arbor

College. Attendance and response showed early signs that small Christian colleges were leaning together toward the distinctive character of integrating faith and learning.

SHIFT #2: FROM DIFFIDENCE TO AFFIRMATION

Momentum toward change took a giant step in 1965 when Carl F. H. Henry invited leaders of Christian higher education to a weekend conference in Washington, DC for the purpose of recasting the image of evangelical Christian colleges. Consistent with Dr. Henry's call for evangelicals to take confidence in our faith and engage our culture, he proposed that we change our identity from being "defenders of the faith" to "faith-affirming" institutions. As editor of *Christianity Today*, Henry summed up "The Faith Affirming College" in his editorial for September 10, 1965:

> The overall purpose of the evangelical college, as a distinct type of institution, is to present the whole truth, with a view to the rational integration of the major fields of learning in the context of the "Judeo-Christian" revelation, and to promote the realization of Christian values in student character.[1]

The editorial went on to spell out the guiding principles and policies to fulfill this basic purpose—theological commitment, trustee composition, faculty selection, integrative instruction, learning resources, church relationship, and student outcomes. While expectations for the "faith-affirming" college were not as rigorous as the imperatives that Henry had demanded for a Christian university focused upon scholarly research, his insistence on presenting the whole truth through the integration of faith and learning as the overall purpose for Christian higher education was the common commitment that would give either institution its distinctive. Yet, the call for transformation from a faith-defending past to a faith-affirming future did not mean a quick fix. Change had to be made in attitude as well as outlook.

SHIFT #3: FROM SELF-DOUBT TO SELF-ESTEEM

As a consultant to evangelical Christian colleges seeking regional accreditation, I often found my first task to be campus-wide attitude adjustment.

---

1. Henry, *Christianity Today*, 25–26.

Trustees, presidents, and faculty all seemed to be peering at the accreditation process through a defensive shield.

In one memorable instance, I started my visit in the president's office. After going over the schedule for consultation, he said, "Let me show you our new science center." As we walked across the campus, I noticed that his steps picked up as we passed a World War II quonset hut where students were streaming in and out. "What's that?" I wondered aloud. The president gave a hurried answer, "Oh, it's just a part of our art program." "Let's go see it," I insisted.

At my mercy, he had no choice. Entering the old hut with its open-studded walls, I saw a fascinating display of violins-in-the-making hanging around the sides. "This is a violin-making class," the president explained, "It is taught by a man of our church who is widely known for his violins, oil paintings, and glass sculptures." "May I meet him?" I asked.

In the next room, the president introduced me to a wizened old man sitting at a large, wooden desk and instructing a student on the art of putting multiple coats of varnish on her violin in order to improve the tone. The science center could wait. I told the president that I would meet him there later and settled into a conversation with a creative genius. After using the violins lining the sides of the hut as an object lesson in his craft, he reached into a lower drawer, pulled out a Stradavarii, and played some bars to demonstrate the purity of its tone. Then, escorting me to another room, he pointed out the products of his oil painting class. With unembellished pride, he talked about the vials of multi-colored powders on a wall shelf that would be mixed into oils. "No commercial paints are used here," he explained. "Every summer I go to the Middle East to choose the purest powder and the most vivid colors for our painting."

By chance, I had discovered the creative center of the campus, but when I commended the president for this unique offering in the Christian college he admitted that he wanted to hurry me past the quonset hut because the master teacher of violin making and oil painting did not have a college degree. When I wrote my report, I recommended that the college proceed with confidence on its self-study for regional accreditation and urged the official visiting team to catch the creative spirit of the campus by becoming acquainted with the old violin-maker.

The Washington conference in 1967 on the "faith-affirming" college caught that same spirit and advanced it to a national level. Evangelical Christian colleges would no longer cower behind the buttressed walls with

a fortress mentality, but would step out into higher education and society
with the good news of an affirming faith.

SHIFT #4:
FROM RESTRICTED PAST TO ALTERNATIVE FUTURES

A year later, in 1967, a grant from the Lilly Endowment made it possible to
convene a consultation at Indiana University to discuss alternative futures
for evangelical Christian higher education. John Snyder, President of the
Bloomington campus of Indiana University, hosted the sessions. Carl F.
H. Henry kicked off with another articulate plea for a Christian university
with a scholarly reputation that would equal Harvard or Johns Hopkins.
Hudson Armerding, President of Wheaton College, followed with a proposal for a university system in which a network of evangelical Christian
colleges would offer a select number of graduate degrees in the fields of
their strength. John Snyder offered a plan for Christian college satellites
adjacent to a major university so that students would have a community
in which they could integrate their university studies with their Christian
faith under the tutelage of resident scholars, along with counsel and fellowship for spiritual growth. Finally, I sketched out a plan for a Christian
College Consortium, especially among those known for the strength of
their commitment to the integration for faith and learning in the Christian liberal arts. Consortium members would be regionally located across
the nation. Their presidents and academic leaders would be committed to
the integrative task, and the institutions would allocate sufficient resources
for start-up costs for the consortium while research and program grants
were being sought from foundations and individuals. The function of the
consortium would be to serve as a think tank for ideas and a laboratory for
pilot studies in cooperative ventures related to the integration of Christian
faith and liberal learning. Once established, the consortium would serve as
a resource center for all of evangelical Christian higher education through
communications, publications, and workshops. Projecting further forward
and connecting with Dr. Henry's proposal for a Christian university, I also
advanced the idea of an Academy of Christian Scholars to honor faculty,
whether in Christian or secular institutions, whose scholarly achievements
qualified them to "challenge the initiative of secular scholars, and to penetrate the collegiate world."

Three of the five presentations resulted in concrete action. Carl Henry never saw his dream for a Christian university realized although he had continued to press his case after planning for the Crusade University in 1960 came to naught. In 1963, he proposed a fund-raising campaign among "Friends of the Christian University" without success, and in 1965 he again outlined the prospects for an International Christian University.[2] As a result of the Indiana consultation, he stepped back from his grand design to establish the Institute for Advanced Christian Studies, a program dedicated to identifying and supporting evangelical Christian scholars whose stature gave them a hearing in the secular university. Henry stated the mission of the IACS, "To enunciate the Christian world-view in order to stem the secular tide that engulfs contemporary culture."[3] Funding from the Lilly Endowment enabled IACS to fund scholars of the stature of Samuel Moffett, Nick Wolterstorff, and Ron Sider as models of the intent for the Christian university.

Hudson Armerding's proposal for a university system of Christian colleges offering graduate degrees in areas of specialty prompted good conversation, but quickly ran aground on the realty that Christian colleges did not have the programs or the resources for offering top quality in postgraduate studies.

John Snyder's plan for a Christian college satellite related to a major university came to fruition when Goshen College developed Conrad Grebel University College, a denominational affiliate, at the University of Waterloo in Ontario, Canada.

My proposal for a Christian College Consortium went back to the drawing board until in 1971 when the idea was tested with a planning grant from the Lilly Endowment through the Institute for Advanced Christian Studies.

The Academy of Christian Scholars stayed on the back burner, perhaps waiting for its time to come.

PARALLEL JOURNEY

A year after the 1967 Indiana University consultation, we moved from Spring Arbor College to the presidency of Seattle Pacific College (now University). My intention was to test the integrative principle in the urban

2. Strachan, *Reenchanting the Evangelical Mind*, 265.
3. Ibid., 267.

setting of Seattle, Washington as it had been tested in the Michigan village. Although worlds apart, the old question of town versus gown had its own challenge for the meaning of the integration of faith and learning. At Spring Arbor, over eighty years of suspicion kept the college and the community apart. This fact came home to me when the local Chevrolet dealer told me that when he was growing up and acting badly, his mother would threaten, "If you don't be good, I am going to send you to Spring Arbor."

THE VILLAGE IS OUR CLASSROOM

Stepping back into history once again, in 1947, the fall of my freshman year at Spring Arbor Junior College, I spotted a beautiful girl walking down the sidelines of the football field. Looking up from my position as quarterback on the intramural football team, I asked my running back who she was. He answered, "She's a Townie." Even though she turned out to be the College pastor's daughter, the label had been stamped her as one of the wild town kids. Today, she is my wife of more than sixty years. Understandably, then, when we returned to Spring Arbor as the President and First Lady of the campus, we invoked the integrative principle and announced that we wanted to make the "Village Our Classroom." With it came the responsibility to serve the community through opportunities for educational, cultural ,and spiritual growth. Because most of our energies went into developing the new four-year college, we made some minor gains, such the Town and Gown cultural series, but had to leave greater progress to our successors.

THE CITY IS OUR CAMPUS

Seattle Pacific College offered the opposite challenge in 1968. Located in the center of enriched educational and cultural resources along with a deep-seated secular attitude, our Christian stance prompted skeptics in the news media to tag the College "the Little Sunday School by the Canal." To counter this misnomer, we announced our intention to make "the city our campus." Rather than competing with the educational and cultural offerings of the metropolis, we utilized these resources to complement the co-curricular climate of the campus. Adopting a strategy of penetration for the city, we urged our students to attend concerts and plays, visit art galleries and historic places, take complementary courses from other universities, and hear the great preachers of the city. At the same time, we tried to lead the way by becoming deeply involved in civic affairs, offered free tuition to senior citizens in our aging neighborhood, and joined with the African-American community in the Central Area to plan a multi-cultural experimental school. The best example of integration between town and gown, however, came with the founding of the School of Business and Economics as part of the transition to university status. In most universities at that time, courses in economics and ethics were offered in departments separate from the School of Business. Following the integrative principle, however, we made economics the liberal arts foundation for business majors and mainstreamed Christian ethics in every course. The Seattle business community responded immediately by recruiting graduates who demonstrated Christian character and professional competence. Today, the spirit of integration is stronger than ever. Alexander Hill and Jeffery Van Duzer, successive deans of the School, have written formative books integrating faith and learning in the fields of business and economics. Hill's book is *Just Business: Christian Ethics for the Marketplace* and Van Duzer's is entitled *Why Business Matters to God (And What Still Needs to Be Fixed)*. Today, in keeping with that integrative thrust, the nationally recognized Center for Integrity in Business stands as the centerpiece that has turned their vision into reality.

THE WORLD IS OUR PARISH

In 1982, we followed the call of God to the presidency of Asbury Theological Seminary in Wilmore, Kentucky, a stopover for Methodist circuit riders during the camp meeting era. Known for its spirit of revivalism and pastors who can preach, Asbury had the heritage of Charles Wesley who spoke of integration with lyrical genius when he prayed, "Let us unite these two, so long divided, learning and vital piety,"[4] and of John Wesley, who responded to ecclesiastical superiors who barred him from preaching in Anglican pulpits by declaring, "I look upon all the world as my parish."[5] To lift the sights of the Seminary from its end of the road and edge of Appalachian setting, we stretched the integrative principle to global dimensions by adopting Wesley's vision as our own and announcing, "The World Is Our Parish." Participation in World Congresses on Evangelism, leadership in the World Methodist Council, faculty exchange with international

4. Parker, *The Heart of John Wesley's Journal*, 55.
5. Outler, *John Wesley*, 72.

seminaries, and agreements with mission societies brought the world to our doorstep. Then, in 1989, the estate gift of Dwight and Lucille Beeson gave us the resources to create the first "smart campus" among theological seminaries so that we could take advantage of the technologies of virtual learning and interactive television on a global scale. The gift also endowed scholarships for international students with the potential for leadership in global ministries.

Each of the Christian college presidents who served in the tumultuous sixties has a similar story to tell. As the culture crumbled, Christ-centered colleges began to rise like a Phoenix bird from the ashes of survival to significance and from diffidence to affirmation. On the fledging wings of a "faith-affirming" identity, we were learning to fly together toward a common on the horizon. Whether in college, university, or seminary, undergraduate or graduate study, village, city, or town, the integrative principle unites faith and learning in the redemptive ways of which August Franke wrote in 1663, "A life changed, a church revived, a nation reformed, a world evangelized."[6] To his words we might well add, "A college reborn."

6. Franke, *Reform, Renewal and Revival.*

9

Cooperative Venture

WHAT HAVE YOU DONE for me lately? The fickle question that voters ask of politicians also applies to public expectations for American higher education. We may think that the academy is immune to fads, but the fact is that higher education is especially vulnerable to passing fashions. Equal opportunity, strategic planning, economic viability, cultural diversity, graduation productivity, social accountability, and global impact are all examples of rising and falling modes in recent years. In the early 1970s, cooperation by consortia had its day, especially in independent higher education. One source identified more than 2,000 consortia being developed or functioning at the time. Strength through cooperation was their common cause. Emphasis tended to be place upon enriched learning opportunities for students, such as international study, cross-disciplinary classes, and exchange programs. Other consortia were founded to make more effective use of resources or join together in fund-raising projects. Still others became research centers providing data on such issues as access, affordability, and assessment as related to public policy.

A TIMELY IDEA

In the early 1970s, Christian higher education also needed an idea whose time had come. The proposal for a Christian College Consortium addressed that need. In its vision there was the potential for cooperative programs, more efficient use of resources, and research on relevant issues, but its primary purpose was the educational philosophy of integrating Christian faith and human learning in the liberal arts. A bold step, indeed, because as Carl Henry and Billy Graham had learned, theological and behavioral differences can be formidable barriers to cooperative action. Could Christian liberal arts colleges come together under the identity as "evangelical" while continuing to hold such theological differences as Reformed, Wesleyan, Mennonite, and Baptist? Would the mutual commitment to advance the integrative principle be greater than the behavioral codes of independent or denominational colleges? The risk had to be tested.

A SELECTIVE INVITATION

After the Indiana University consultation in 1967, a series of conversations with Charles Williams—my former Vice-President of Advancement at Spring Arbor College and then Director for Religion at Lilly Endowment—began to shape a proposal that met the interest of the Endowment and addressed the needs of evangelical Christian liberal arts colleges. Our debate centered on the question of whether to initiate a national association on Christian higher education or to create a smaller group that could pretest cooperative ideas around the integration of faith and learning. We finally agreed that the institutions invited to the first planning session should be limited in number, academically strong, regionally selected, financially viable, and led by a president who actively promoted the integration of faith and learning in the Christian liberal arts. Other schools of equal or greater academic strength might have been chosen, but the limits of the grant and the desire to create a national network of regional representatives guided the final selection.

On this basis, then, Lilly Endowment supported a planning grant of $25,000 through the Institute for Advanced Christian Studies to test the viability of the idea. Fourteen presidents of Christian colleges received an invitation to attend a planning conference in December, 1970 at Tempe, Arizona. Invitees representing various regions of the nation were: Asbury College, Bethel College, Calvin College, Eastern Mennonite College, Gordon College, Greenville College, Houghton College, Malone College, Messiah College, Oklahoma Christian College, Seattle Pacific College, Taylor University, Westmont College, and Wheaton College. Eleven responded favorably, two (Calvin and Oklahoma Christian) turned down the invitation, and Eastern Mennonite initially deferred pending further consideration.

Robert Sandin, Professor of Higher Education at the University of Toledo, served as a planning consultant and championed the idea of creating a university system among the colleges, perhaps as a prelude to Dr. Henry's dream of a national Christian university.

Consistent with the purpose of the grant, I sent out the letter with the call to the conference. It read, in part:

> We need to define the contemporary purpose of the evangelical Christian college and related programs in the ministry of the church. The definition would have to be theologically sound, educationally meaningful, and socially responsible. It would have to be firm enough to stand the test of history, but flexible enough to meet the surprises of the future.

Following is a sampling of the affirmative responses from presidents who accepted the invitation:

> The Christian College Consortium is an act of pioneering in Christian education. The time has come for innovation, for courageous action, for advance thinking in reference to our Christian colleges . . .
>
> Harold J. Ockenga, President,
> Gordon College

> We acknowledge the need for cooperative action, and we believe in the potential strength of group action. I am happy to join the other ten presidents in a program to accomplish the objectives of the CCC.
>
> Milo A. Rediger, President
> Taylor University

> We see in the Christian College Consortium a vehicle for getting visibility in society for this kind of education and its validity which acting individually and alone we cannot produce.
>
> Everertt L. Cattell, President
> Malone College

> The Christian College Consortium is the product of necessity and opportunity. Rapidly rising costs and the vigorous challenge of public higher education have made it imperative for the Christian college to avoid needless duplication of programs and the isolation that too often condemns an institution to a provincialism or isolationism that fails to profit from the collective experience of others.
>
> Hudson T. Armerding, President
> Wheaton College

> The new Christian College Consortium is a significant step forward in creating a network of association between our Christian colleges across the nation. While many of the benefits may accrue to the students, it should also follow that those of us in administration and the teaching faculty should be enriched as well by serious in-depth dialogue which relates a Christian world view to contemporary issues.
>
> Myron S. Augsburger, President
> Eastern Mennonite College

On the strength of these responses, plans for the Tempe Conference went forward with confidence that Christian colleges were poised for a breakthrough in cooperative action around a common cause.

MOMENT OF TRUTH

The dynamics of the Tempe meeting are still fresh in my mind. As might be expected, each of the plenary speakers brought their particular perspective to the Consortium idea. Earl McGrath, despite his earlier warning about the Christian colleges becoming as extinct as the whooping crane, foresaw cooperation as a means to increase the visibility and viability of evangelical Christian colleges on the national scene. Carl F. H. Henry took his familiar position of seeing faith-affirming colleges unified in advancing apologetics and evangelism. Nels Ferre, the philosopher, was also invited, but could not attend because of illness. He sent a dreary word, however, by likening of Christian colleges to "little islands adrift in the mainstream of American higher education."[1]

Getting down to specifics, William Jellema applied the findings of his Association of American College study, *From Red to Black? Special Preliminary Report on the Financial Status, Present and Projected, of Private Institutions of Higher Learning*, to small Christian colleges with limited financial support. His conclusion triggered the need for cooperation in a dramatic way. Jellema's study focused on the financial viability of small, independent colleges. While most of these schools were balancing budgets and even growing in enrollments, he discovered the fragile underpinnings of what we now call "enrollment-driven, tuition-supported, and aid dependent" institutions. Endowments and reserve funds were severely limited and annual fund-raising efforts contributed a very small percentage to overall

---

1. Ferre, personal letter, 1971.

operational need. Therefore, just the slightest shift in enrollment numbers, tuition costs. or financial aid could tip the balanced budgets of small, independent college into deficit operations pushing on the margins of survival.[2]

Among all of the indicators for assessing the financial viability of independent college and universities in 1969–70, Jellema discovered one that stood out. The size of the gap between tuition costs and institutionally-funded student aid (net tuition revenue) correlated directly with the financial health of the institution. Jellema saw this problem escalating on a spiral of increasing tuition requiring more and more student financial aid as the basis for increasing enrollment. In 1970–71, Jellema repeated his study again and found that deficits in net tuition revenues had increased 26 percent. Bluntly, but realistically, Jellema predicted that if the size of the deficit in net tuition revenue continued to grow, 25 percent or more of private colleges would cease to exist.

Although the 11 presidents attending the planning meeting for the CCC represented schools that were relatively strong in financial operations, none of them fit the special category of "endowed institutions" with investment earnings filling in the gap between tuition costs and student financial aid. Wheaton and Messiah had shared an endowment gift that made them the strongest among the participants, but even they still faced the dilemma of rising tuition rates and the need for increasing student financial aid. After Jellema compared the financial status of our colleges with the findings of his national survey, he spoke the prophetic words, "Frail reeds, when bound together, must be bound tightly."

Every president in the room paid heed to these words. We needed centering truth in Jesus Christ to come together in the spirit of cooperation. We also needed to generate a critical mass of evangelical Christian colleges around this spirit in order to assure viability.

At that time, another metaphor came into our conversation. We concluded that the integration of faith and human learning in the Christian liberal arts was the "hook on which we would hang our hats."

Each of the presidents went home to reflect upon this commitment, test it with their boards and their faculties, and make a decision of whether or not to become bound together with their colleagues as a member of the Christian College Consortium.

2. Jellema, *From Red to Black?*, xi.

A RUNNING START

Events moved rapidly to the formal organization of the Christian College Consortium: Ten presidents of the eleven original respondents enrolled their institutions as charter members; an executive committee was formed with David McKenna (Chair), Carl Lundquist (Vice-Chair), Milo Rediger (Secretary/Treasurer); and Hudson Armerding and Ray Hostetter as Members-at-Large; Dr. Edward Neteland was named as the first Executive Director; incorporation in the State of Indiana followed on July 1, 1971, and the IACS grant of $22,000 was continued along with $15,000 from member institutions and $16,000 as gifts for basic operations.

An ambitious set of nine goals had to be sorted for priorities in the first year of the CCC:

1. To promote the purposes of evangelical Christian higher education within the church and society;

2. To present a strong rationale for the role of evangelical Christian higher education today;

3. To encourage cooperation among evangelical Christian colleges;

4. To encourage and support scholarly research among Christian scholars on the integration of faith and learning;

5. To initiate programs which will improve the quality of instruction and encourage innovation in member institutions;

6. To research the educational effectiveness of member institutions with particular emphasis upon student development;

7. To improve the management efficiency of member institutions;

8. To expand the human, financial, and material resources available to member institutions; and

9. To explore the feasibility of a university system.

In its first year of the Consortium, under the leadership of Dr. Neteland, special attention was given to the ninth goal of exploring the idea of a university system of Christian Colleges as a feasible option for the future. Dr. Neteland proposed a five-year plan directed toward that goal. In Phase I (1971–72) CCC would be established; in Phase II (1972–75), the CCC would be expanded as an Association of Christian Colleges; and in Phase III (1975 forward) the university system of Christian colleges would be put in place. After exploration, however, the plan was put aside as premature because the Consortium needed time to test its fledging wings and prove that it could fly.

A SENSE OF DIRECTION

Revision of Dr. Neteland's five-year plan did not deter the CCC from taking major steps toward the goal of advancing the integration of faith and learning as the educational essence of the evangelical Christian college. Dr. Neteland led the way in coordinating the first Institute on Faith and Learning in August, 1972 for 37 faculty participants and publishing a Consortium newsletter under the title *Universitas*. Other cooperative programs progressed through planning stages during this first year, such as developing reciprocal tuition grants for faculty children of CCC schools; initiating faculty exchange for summer schools; and proposing a cost-saving property and casualty insurance package for CCC members.

As the exploration for a focused purpose moved past the university system and beyond some of the more ambitious goals for cooperation, the integration of faith and learning came to top again and again. In a special issue of *Universitas*, published in March, 1972, I, as Chair of the CCC Board, wrote an appeal for all Christian colleges to make the integration of faith and learning the primary reason for their existence and the legitimate claim for their distinctive role in American higher education. More than forty years later, the passion for that position burns brighter than ever.

10

Compelling Insight

ELTON TRUEBLOOD WROTE, "A Christian is a person who is willing to bet his life that Christ is right."[1] Can we make the same bold statement about the integration of faith and learning as the distinguishing character and distinctive contribution of the Christian college in American higher education? Needless to say, it is a gamble because of the complexity and controversy surrounding the subject. Yet, the concept itself is firmly grounded in the theology, philosophy, and history of the Christian higher education. Formative insights from each of these areas set the stage for discussion of the challenges that go along with our commitment to the integrative concept.

THEOLOGICAL FOUNDATIONS

All higher education professes to be search for truth. Christian higher education is a part of that search, but it also lays claim to the discovery of truth. Biblically-based foundations undergird our search and discovery.

"All truth is God's truth," the premise advanced by Arthur Holmes traces back through the theology of Augustine to the Biblical account of Creation:

---

1. Trueblood, *A Place to Stand*, 60

He is the image of the invisible God, the firstborn over all creation. For by him all things were created: things in heaven and on
earth, visible and invisible, whether thrones or powers or rulers
or authorities: all things were created by him and for him. (Col
1:15–16)

A corollary truth immediately follows. "All truth is God's truth" as
preceded, centered, and cohered in Jesus Christ:

He is before all things, and in him all things hold together (Col
1:17).

Christ himself then takes us the next step in understanding "All truth
as God's truth" when He promises the Spirit of Truth who:

. . . will teach you all things and remind you of everything that I
said to you . . . (John 14:26).

. . . will convict the world of guilt in regard to sin and righteousness and judgment . . . (John 16.3).

. . . and will tell you what is yet to come (John 16:3).

The Holy Spirit, as the agent of all truth, uses the instrument of the
inspired Word of God as the text for his teaching:

All Scripture is God-breathed and is useful for teaching, rebuking, correcting, and training in righteousness, so that the man of
God may be thoroughly equipped for every good work (2 Tim
3:16–17).

The integration of faith and learning, then, is grounded in these four foundational premises:

1. All truth is God's truth.

2. All truth is centered in Christ.

3. All truth is taught by Holy Spirit.

4. All truth is written in the Word of God.

In these truths we see Christian scholarship as one of the highest call-
ings of God. A Christian scholar is a person called to a search and discovery
mission, unlimited in God's creation, centered in Christ, led by the Holy
Spirit, and informed by the Word of God.

Contrary to critics who claim that Christian scholarship is an oxy-
moron, this definition does not close down intellectual inquiry with

non-negotiable answers to every question. Yes, the integration of faith and learning will result in discoveries of God's truth about realities and finalities that cannot be compromised. But, in the search and discovery process itself, the Christian scholar who holds these premises will be most confident in asking all questions, most respectful in hearing all options, and most humble in saying, "I don't know." Robert Wuthnow lifts the vocation of Christian scholarship to its highest level of meaning when he writes that "Christianity *sacralizes*—makes-sacred—the intellectual life. It gives the questions we struggle with in our work and in our lives a larger significance."[2]

Glib acceptance of these truths falls far short of reality. The Apostle Paul likens our task to intellectual warfare in which we are conquerors, not by using weapons of force or claiming triumphal victories, but by the self-discipline of ideas:

> Our war is not fought with weapons of flesh, yet they are strong enough, in God's cause, to demolish fortresses. We demolish soph-
> istries, and the arrogance that resists the knowledge of God; every
> thought is our prisoner, captured to be brought into obedience to
> Jesus Christ. (2 Cor 10:4–5)

When we review these truths in the context of integrating Christian faith and human learning, we understand why Elton Trueblood said, "It is the vocation of the Christian intellectual to be both tough-minded and tender-hearted, and to be both at once."[3] Hard truth and a humble spirit become one whenever we venture into the realm of God's truth.

PHILOSOPHICAL FOUNDATIONS

The intellectual history of Christianity is rich with the thinking of Christian scholars in every generation who continue to explore the educational implications of the premise, "All truth is God's Truth," a philosophical statement that includes natural as well as special revelation. The late Arthur Holmes stands out as one of the great minds and spirits who centered on this question. Like the Matterhorn rising out the mist, Holmes shows us the peak of philosophical thought about the Christian college:

---

2. Wuthnow, *Christianity in the Twenty-First Century*, 209, 211, 212.

3. Trueblood, *A Place to Stand*, 36.

To confess God as Creator and Christ as Lord is thus to affirm his hand in all life and thought. It is to admit that every part of the created order is sacred, and the Creator calls us to exhibit his wisdom and power both by exploring the creating and developing it resources and by bringing our own created abilities to fulfillment. For while all nature declares the glory of God, we men uniquely image the Creator in our created creativity. Implicit in the doctrine of creation is a cultural mandate and a call to creative integration of faith with intellect, not just to preserve biblical studies in our school, but more basically to see every area of thought and life in relation to the wisdom and will of God and to replenish the earth with the creativity of human art and science.[4]

Bernard Ramm, in his book, *The Christian College in the Twentieth Century,* discovers these same principles at work in the thoughts and writings of Aurelius Augustine, Philip Melancthon, John Henry Newman, Abraham Kuyper, and Sir Walter Moberly. Summing up his findings, Ramm gives us a philosophically-based framework for the twentieth-century Christian university:

1. A university is Christian only as it is Christian throughout;

2. A Christian university has the liberal arts at the center of its curriculum;

3. A Christian university, within the common grace of God, shares in the transmission of the culture;

4. A Christian university relates itself vitally to the Christian Church;

   a. The Church must recognize the necessity of scholarship and academic freedom within the university;

   b. The Church must be careful regarding its Creed;

   c. The professor must not confuse freedom of speech with academic freedom;

   d. The professor must realize that academic freedom is also a set of responsibilities; and

   e. If the gift to the professor by the Church and the university is academic freedom, the gifts of the professor to the Church and the university is integrity.[5]

4. Holmes, *The Idea of a Christian College,* 29.

5. Ramm, *The Christian College in the Twentieth Century,* 115–23.

Readers of Ramm's book will be quick to note the subsets to his final point. Pointedly, he identifies the faculty of the Christian university as gate-keepers of theological and philosophical integrity. In this thought, the oft-quoted word of Father John Hesburgh of Notre Dame comes to mind, "The university is the place where the Church does its thinking."[6] For good reason, the primacy of the professor, the integrity of the university, and its relationship to the church came front and center in the developmental stages of the Christian College Consortium.

Historically, ever since Jesus resisted the acclaim of Greek scholars (John 12:20–33) and Paul addressed the Greek philosophers at Mars Hill (Acts 1:22–31), Christians have been asking, "What has Jerusalem to do with Athens?" In answer to this question, Origen established what might be considered the first Christian liberal arts college in the third century. As his clerical assignment, Origen was appointed to teach the scriptures to students in the ecclesiastical school located in Alexandria, Egypt. With its renowned library and museum, the city stood at the intellectual and historical crossroads of the ancient world. Origen, rather than remaining cloistered in his ecclesiastical school, took his faith into debate with pagan philosophers in the Alexandrian library. For instance, when a book entitled *Against the Christians* circulated like a best-seller among the intelligentsia of the Roman Empire, Origen countered his own book, *Against Celsus*, to refute the charges, especially that Christian beliefs contradicted the sciences.[7]

Out of this experience, Origen's idea for the academy took a revolutionary turn. Origen broadened the curriculum to include courses in literature, arts, and sciences as well as scripture. At the risk of censure and even death, he put these learning sources through the discipline of textual criticism, reading, interpretation, and judgment.[8] One of Origen's students named Gregory wrote a letter under the title *Address to Origen* in which he commends his teacher for integrating theory and practice, not just to learn about the principles of morality, but to exercise those virtues themselves.[9] Creative teaching led students to that goal. Origen would often present pagan philosophies with a serious tone and Christian doctrines in a less

6. University of Notre Dame blog network, ". . . Where the Catholic Church Does Its Thinking," posted November 11, 2011.

7. The Gregorian Institute of Benedictine College, blog, January 9, 2012.

8. Trigg, *Origen*, 6.

9. Ibid., 37.

serious way so that his students would have to grapple with the differences for themselves before hearing the convictions of their tutor. By this means, Gregory sees the ideal of Christ in Origen's teaching. He wants "to transform his disciples into his own likeness."[10]

In a very real sense, the concept of integrating Christian faith and human learning was born. Then, as his students advanced in integrative understanding, he challenged them to test their faith, without prejudice, against the conflicting ideas of other philosophies. For those who reached advanced levels of scholarship, he dared them to test them in the white-hot crucible of personal confrontation with pagan philosophers in the library at Alexandria.

Following Origen's lead, we can envision a model for the future of the Christian liberal arts college: (1) a curriculum designed for the *integration* of divine revelation with human reason; (2) instruction leading to *differentiation* between Christian and secular worldviews; and 3) scholarship on faith and learning issues for *contention* in the halls of the secular academy. Whether in the ancient world when Christian faith encountered Greek thought or in the contemporary setting of asking how Christian faith related to the empirical evidence of scientific discovery, these same three goals apply.

John R.W. Stott echoed these thoughts as a fervent prayer in his book, *Your Mind Matters:*

> I pray earnestly that God will raise up today a new generation of Christian apologists or Christian communicators, who will combine an absolute loyalty to the biblical gospel and the unwavering confidence in the power of the Spirit with a deep and sensitive understanding of the contemporary alternatives to the gospel; who will relate the one to the other with freshness, pungency, authority and relevance; and who will use *their* minds to reach *other* minds for Christ.[11]

The call of these esteemed leaders of the past has been answered by a host of established scholars writing books on the theology, history, and philosophy of the Christian college and university. Within these volumes, there is no lack of sophisticated intellect at work on the specific question of integrating faith and learning. It is especially gratifying to look on a bookshelf and see the names and titles of contemporary scholars who dig deeply into the

10. Ibid., 38.

11. Stott, *Your Mind Matters*, 52.

meaning of the Christian college in American higher education. Stalwarts such as George Marsden, Nathan Hatch, Mark Noll, Joel Carpenter, David Wells, and Nick Wolsterstorff stand tall among their secular peers as well as among other Christian colleagues in their respective fields. Equally gratifying is to note the books and articles specifically dedicated to the integration of faith and learning that have been written by presidents, deans, and faculty members while serving in Christian College Consortium schools— Gayle Beebe, Philip Eaton, Michael Hamilton, Harold Heie, Ray Hostetter, Duane Liftin, Karen Longman, James Mannoia, Michael Peterson, Steve Moore, Kenneth Myers, and others.[12]

Mark Noll's book, *Jesus Christ and the Life of the Mind*, is a prime example of the serious thinking about the integration of faith and learning that has continued with new energy into the twenty-first century. Building on the pillar of Christology in scripture and the historic creeds, he draws out four expectations for integration in the intellectual life of the Christian scholar—doubleness, contingency, particularity, and self-denial.[13] With his usual succinctness, Noll sums up these four expectations in the statement:

> Scholarship that is keyed expressly to the person and the work of Christ will not disoriented by confronting the paradoxical or the mysterious; it will always be more comfortable in what comes to the mind from outside than in what the mind concludes on its own; it will realize the value of particulars because of Christian universals; and it will be humble, charitable, self-giving, and modest.[14]

His summary of these expectations could well be etched over the entrance to every Christian college.

Returning to our interpretation of Origen's model for integration, differentiation, and contention, how did the Christian College Consortium address these progressive goals? Integration in the curriculum of the Christian liberal arts became the obvious starting point. Priority was given to the development of a Faith/Learning Institute that would bring together senior and junior professors from Consortium colleges in order to tap and transmit the experience of integrative teaching. If effective, the outcome of integrative and incarnational teaching would be differentiation of the Christian worldview from secular perspectives as a basis for living and serving as

12. See bibliography.

13. Noll, *Jesus Christ and the Life of the Mind*, 43–64

14. Ibid., 64.

well as learning. Until the goals of integration and differentiation were achieved, contention in the secular academy, perhaps through Carl Henry's dream of a Christian university, would have to remain a future prospect. The presidents who came together under the aegis of the Christian College Consortium kept each of these goals in mind. Progression from integration to differentiation to contention is the model that will bring the Christian college to full maturity. Having concluded that sound scholarship has given us the theological, historical, and philosophical groundwork for this model and that integration is the starting point, our challenge shifts from sound thinking to effective practice. Here's where the rub comes in.

FROM IDEA TO IMPLEMENTATION

To demonstrate our commitment to the idea of integration, a Faith/Learning Institute in the summer of 1972 became our first order of business for the newly developed Christian College Consortium. The Institute convened at North Park College in Chicago, under the direction of Melvin Lorentzen, Professor of Creative Writing and Communications at Wheaton College.[15] Dr. Lorentzen brought with his leadership the advantage of having participated in the Faith/Learning faculty workshops at Wheaton inaugurated by Arthur Holmes in the 1960s. Invitations went out to each of the Consortium colleges to send faculty representatives to the Institute. All eleven member schools responded and a total of thirty-seven faculty members participated. Four specific goals were set as starting points: (1) to define "faith" and "learning"; (2) to identify key issues in the integration of faith and learning; (3) to investigate the integrative process within and across disciplines; and (4) to plan for continuing integration on campuses and in future workshops. When the participants were asked to evaluate progress toward these goals in the sessions, they felt as if the first two goals were achieved, but gave a mixed review on the last two goals with the specific notation that the discussions on integration across disciplines tended to be either too little or too much. Unanimously, they noted that writing a paper on integration in their field of study proved to be a most valuable experience. While recognizing the contribution of lectures and counsel from distinguished scholars outside the Consortium colleges, the participants discovered that they had resources within their own ranks that needed to be tapped in future institutes.

15. Lorentzen, "Final Report on the Faith/Learning Institute," 1972.

Two additional insights came from the evaluations. One was to see the need for bringing younger and newer faculty to the Institute. Most of the participants were senior scholars who had already established their own methods for integrative teaching in their discipline. Younger scholars, especially in the first years of their careers, would benefit most from interaction with senior scholars.

The other insight revealed the need for some form of theological education for the faculties of Consortium colleges. Few of the participants had academic degrees or formal courses in theology. Because integration depends upon strength of understanding in both theology and the scholar's discipline, the participants urged Consortium colleges to assist faculty members in developing their own "biblical perspectives on their disciplines, and to devise effective ways of communicating these to their students in and out of lecture halls and laboratories."[16] With unanimous agreement, the thirty-seven professors commended the value of the Institute, recommended its continuation in the future, and urged the deans of the respective schools to be a part of the program. Time did not permit the participants to discuss in depth the issues that they identified as challenges for the integrative process. Subjects such as curricular reform, instructional innovation, faculty development, and assessment of outcomes were reserved for a future Faith/Learning Institute. It is to these issues that we now turn.

16. Ibid., 3.

11

Dauntless Task

CAN CHRISTIAN COLLEGES SUCCEED where some of the greatest universities in the world have failed? Ever since medieval universities adopted the *trivium* and *quadrivium* as the core for the classical curriculum, institutions of higher education have been chasing after the Holy Grail of liberal learning in changing times. We have already seen how the faculty of Harvard has gone through periodic spasms in attempts to develop a core curriculum in General Education. Without agreement on the source of truth, there is no center to hold the curriculum together. So, the quest goes on.

THE CHALLENGE OF CURRICULAR REFORM

Regular as clockwork, Christian colleges go through periods of curricular reform to correct and redefine the meaning of the Christian liberal arts. Natural erosion of the core curriculum comes from both internal and external pressures. For one, the knowledge industry is racing at blinding speed in every field of study. The scene has been likened to playing baseball with a moveable left field fence so that yesterday's home run becomes today's easy out. Another metaphor envisions the scholar trying to shoot a flying bird using a .22 caliber rifle while balancing on the deck of a speeding boat. In either case, a scholar who wants to keep pace with new knowledge has more than a full-time job. Even if a researcher comes to an integrative insight or a teacher develops a module with integrative learning as the goals, the field keeps moving on with more and more unanswered intellectual, moral, and social questions. As one skeptic noted, "We are learning more and more about less and less so that soon we will know nothing."

Another pressure comes as knowledge expands and specialization increases. To keep pace with their field faculty members are pressed to focus their attention on a special area of study and offer additional courses reflecting that interest. Even in Christian colleges where faculty members enjoy personal relationships with colleagues across schools and departments, interdisciplinary research and cooperative studies suffer.

Careerism, bolstered by accreditation in professional fields, is an archenemy of a core curriculum in the Christian liberal arts. In order to meet the demands of the professional field, required courses give way to lesser options and specialized courses take over the first two years of the college experience at the expense of general education. Every president and dean of a Christian college or university has a horror story to tell about the pressure to compromise the core curriculum in the Christian liberal arts in order to meet the demands of professional specialization. My own horrific story comes from an exit interview with the chair of the visiting committee for accreditation with the National League of Nursing. She told me that our accreditation depended upon an earlier start on professional courses for nursing students along with a radically reduced faculty-student ratio. When I complained that the requirements cut into our core curriculum in the Christian liberal arts and undercut the faculty-student ratio of our strategic plan, she answered, "We are talking about a life and death matter. It's up to you."

Graduate studies further compound the problem because students are expected to go narrow and deep in their studies. Little or no time is left from the demands of course work, comprehensives, and dissertation to stop and weigh the implications of their learning for their Christian faith. Likewise, very few doctoral programs include courses in college teaching that might touch upon integrative principles and process. Consequently, most recruits for teaching positions in Christian colleges and universities come in with limited knowledge of teaching skills and even more limited knowledge of teaching for the integration of faith and learning.

THE CHALLENGE OF INSTRUCTIONAL INNOVATION

Learning to teach for the integration of faith and learning takes time and creativity. Faculty participants in the first Faith/Learning Institute of the CCC brought with them deep convictions and enthusiastic readiness to delve into the subject at hand. Reality, however, checked in early. Because of heavy loads of teaching and advising, along with extra-curricular expectations, time for reflecting upon the integrative process, developing integrative courses, and testing integrative teaching in the classroom was severely limited. Yet, in the cracks of discretionary time, they did it. Without any common pattern for integrative teaching, each faculty member revealed his or her individualized approach to the question. The result was not chaotic, but it was piecemeal. I know how they felt. Every candidate whom I interviewed for a position in Christian higher education enthusiastically embraced the opportunity to integrate their faith with their field. After being hired, however, they are often left on their own. When this happens, new faculty members will find various ways in which to express their faith through their teaching. Some may assume that prayer at the beginning of the class will sanctify a lecture that might be given in any institution of higher learning. Others will let their testimony suffice as evidence of their commitment as a Christian scholar. Still others will adopt a split world approach to learning, either bringing biblical insights alongside content from their field or laying out discoveries from their field and then trumping them with biblical proof texts. One might assume that faculty scholars will outgrow these limited choices. Experience, however, shows that early patterns tend to persist. Without some kind of intervention for teaching how to teach and teaching how to integrate faith and learning, senior faculty will tend to do the same thing that they did in their early years, except with better understanding of their field, more maturity in their faith, and greater wisdom in working with students.

THE CHALLENGE OF FACULTY DEVELOPMENT

Our dilemma deepens when we remember that the integration of faith and learning requires a sound knowledge base on each side of the equation. Few Christian scholars have the same depth of biblical knowledge and understanding that they have for their field of specialization. Even life-long students of the Word may feel as if their lack of theological education is a handicap. Perhaps this is why teachers depend upon prayer, witness, and role modeling as their contribution to integrative teaching. Without confidence in a sound biblical base to match their disciplinary knowledge, they are reluctant to delve into the realm where there are no easy answers or formulas where one size fits all.

We may be failing to utilize one of the special resources of the Christian college, namely, its religion faculty. With just a little imagination, we can envision these scholars not touting theology as the "queen of the sciences," but seeing themselves as "servants of the sciences" assisting their colleagues in the biblical dimension of integration in the curriculum and in instruction. The religion faculty, as well as the faculty of any other discipline, can hunker down in the splendid isolation of their own specialization. In one extreme case, a young faculty member under scrutiny for tenure spoke of her strong interest in the integration of faith and learning in her scientific field. A religion professor on the committee rebuffed her because she lacked the theological credentials necessary to the integrative process. She left discouraged. But what a contribution the religion professor could have made to her personal and professional growth if he had said, "If I can help you, let me know." His comments also bare the fact that the institution had not declared its intention to make integration the centerpiece of its identity or communicate the integrative spirit throughout its ranks. Christian colleges and universities need a full-scale plan for faculty development in the integrative process, beginning with the initial identification of faculty prospects and progressing through the decisions of promotion, tenure, and the honors of retirement.

THE CHALLENGE OF TRANSFORMATIONAL ASSESSMENT

If you read the ads for Christian colleges and universities, you will find no hesitancy in claiming an educational experience that results in transformational change for the student, not just intellectually, but morally and spiritually as well. Furthermore, the ads go on to claim that graduates will be agents of transformation for changing the world. As much as we want to believe these claims, our evidence is thin. This is not to take away from the stories of alumni whose lives were transformed by the experience of Christian higher education or those who are making a profound impact upon the field of service to which they are called. But, at the time of the founding of the CCC assessment based on qualitative research into the outcomes of learning in the Christian liberal arts, especially in the area of integration, was like a new frontier waiting to be explored.

Limited research gave us some hints about transformational outcomes. Available results leaned toward the pessimistic conclusion of "selection in; graduation out" with little change between. Might we also say, "character in; character out" for students in Christian higher education with little change between? Schools that admit only committed Christians may be more honest in recognizing the limits of transformational change in the Christian college experience. Their assumption is that the Christian college or university is most effective in refining the character created in the home and redeemed by faith in Jesus Christ. Others, who admit non-Christians, take on greater responsibility as evangelism becomes part of their educational mission. Either case can be supported by individual testimonies of students whose lives have been changed. To confirm, change or deny these assumptions requires extensive research into the impact of the Christian college experience on the belief, being, and behavior of its graduates in comparison with their secular peers. Admittedly, assessment of integrative teaching and learning is most difficult because the primary outcomes are qualitative, not quantitative. Standard measures of educational outcomes are helpful, but not complete. Highly sophisticated instruments of research must be developed to assess the claim of transformational change in the Christian college and university. Ultimately, of course, each institution will have to customize its instruments according to its mission, its culture, and its claims. From its very beginning, the Consortium was perceived as a vehicle to lead the way in such a front-edge venture.

THE CCC RESPONSE

All of these persistent challenges surfaced in the conversation of the Consortium's first Faith/Learning Institute. At the end, the conclusion could be drawn that the integration of faith and learning, the distinguishing character of Christian higher education, is at one and the same time, eloquently written in history, theology, and philosophy, but short of implementation in curricular reform, instructional innovation, integrative teaching, and transformational assessment. Whoever said, "It takes ten years for a new idea in higher education to get from the drawing board to the classroom" did not miss the timing by much. Our work was cut out for us.

Under the leadership of Dr. Edward Neteland, first Executive Director of the CCC, the goal for integrating faith and learning received strong support through: (a) publication of *Universitas* dedicated to dialogue on integrative issues across the CCC campuses and beyond; (b) establishment of a Dean's Council for cooperative curriculum development and guidance for the Faith/Learning Institute; and (c) introduction of the Distinguished Scholar Lectureship at CCC colleges, beginning with John R.W. Stott.

At the same time, Dr. Neteland's entrepreneurial vision for a university system of Christian colleges turned to disappointment when exploration revealed that the academic strengths of the institutions, especially at the graduate level, did not coalesce into a scholarly network at the required level of excellence. Dr. Neteland's dream for a National Association of Christian higher within a five-year period also seemed premature when the CCC was still in its start-up stages. Plans for a national conference on inter-institutional cooperation, a national congress on Christian higher education, and a national multi-media program promoting Christian colleges also had to be set aside in favor of the focus upon the issues related to the integration of faith and learning. After serving two years as Executive Director/President, Dr. Neteland resigned his position early in 1973. The parting was amicable, but left the question of leadership up in the air. Would our infant organization die an early death? To whom would we turn?

PART 3

Gathering Speed

"A movement has momentum when a commanding truth becomes its driving force."

12

Stutter Step

WHILE STILL ON FLEDGING legs, the Christian College Consortium hit a stutter step. Dr. Neteland's resignation sent the CCC presidents back to the drawing board to rewrite the expectations for leadership that would take the organization into the future. In order to conduct a thorough search for the new President/Executive Director, the Executive Committee opted to take a year for the process. I agreed to serve as the interim CEO and bring the CCC office to Seattle Pacific College until the new leader was elected. While honoring the limits of interim leadership, we knew that the initial momentum of the CCC had to be maintained or it stood the chance of early death. Plans to continue the Faith/ Learning Institute along with the publication of *Universitas* took top priority. Four other lines of action were taken to bridge the gap and keep alive the spirit of hope that brought the CCC into existence.

PRESIDENTIAL LEADERSHIP

As the qualifications for presidential leadership were being rewritten to guide the search for the new President/Executive Director, the focus shifted toward the academic qualifications for advancing the integration of faith and learning on the campus and in the sector of Christian higher education. We sought a person with a PhD in an academic field, a background in the history, theology, and philosophy of integration, specific experience in implementing the concept at a Christian college, and the stature to serve as our spokesperson in both the Christian and secular academies. These qualifications fit the growing strength of the Dean's Council in cooperative curricular development on CCC campuses along with its planning and direction for the Faith/ Learning Institute. Our new President/Executive Director needed the academic credentials and experience to win the confidence of the deans as well as the presidents in CCC leadership.

INTEGRATIVE PROCESS

When faculty from the CCC colleges gathered for the first Faith/Learning Institute, they brought with them any number of individualized approaches to the integrative process. As noted earlier, their commitment to the concept was strong and their interest in its development was enthusiastic. But, they lacked a common process to guide their scholarship toward integration across diverse and highly specialized fields. Without assuming to have all of the answers, we re-emphasized Bernard Ramm's paradigm that brought biblical revelation into dialogue with human knowledge in order to discover where and when the two ways of knowing truth *converged* in agreement, *diverged* in conflict, or *emerged* as perplexing questions for continuing research. No attempt was made to force feed this process into all fields or with all professors, but it did give a starting point for conversation. Even more important, it gave the opening to reinforce the fact that the process depended upon faculty understanding of both revealed Truth and discovered truth, or the scriptures and the faculty members' specific disciplines.

CHRISTIAN WORLDVIEW

Discussion in the first Faith/Learning Institute also opened up the question about teaching from and to a Christian worldview. The integration of faith and learning assumes a Christian worldview that stands alone among all other perspectives. In the dialogue between biblical revelation and human knowledge, the question of worldview becomes all-important. Behind every fact, theory, or hypothesis, there is a perspective on truth that encompasses the meaning of all existence, whether physical, organic, or human. Secularists who scoff at the Christian's premise, "All truth is God's truth," are not honest until they confess that their central premise is, "All truth is man's truth." Even relativists who deny absolute truth should be honest enough to admit their own absolute, "All truth is relative truth." From this central premise, the lines of interpretation extend to every aspect of life, learning, living, and dying.

Kenneth Boulding, in his book, *The Meaning of the Twentieth Century: The Great Transition,* says that a worldview has three parts:

> An *interpretation of human history* that unfolds before us as convincing drama in which we find our role;
>
> A *moral standard or system of values* by which to judge truth and error in our human knowledge, good and evil in our human behavior; and
>
> A *vision of the future* that is significant, exciting and positive, and in which we see our part.[1]

Futurists follow this same pattern by basing their predictions upon the processes of synthesizing, norming, and futuring.[2] Synthesizing is integrating new information into our interpretation of human history; norming is the process of setting moral standards for guiding human behavior in changing times; and futuring is the vision of the future in which we find our hope.

As we began to explore the Christian worldview within this framework, Jesus' promise of the Holy Spirit took on new meaning. When Jesus introduced his Holy Spirit as the one would "lead us into all truth," he gave us the synthesizing Spirit who would bring all new information into focus through his interpretation of history. In the words, "When he (the Spirit of Truth) is come, he will convict the world of sin, righteousness and judgment," Jesus gave us the norming Spirit who set the moral standard for judging right and wrong, good and evil. Then, with an eye on our future, Jesus said that the Holy Spirit would show us "things to come" and serve as the futuring Spirit in whom we find our role and our hope in a fast-changing world.

The prospect for developing a Christian worldview as an educational outcome for teaching and learning in the Christian college and university becomes a very real possibility through this process. But it cannot be achieved without understanding that Jesus Christ is the one who "holds all things together." Therefore, Boulding's paradigm for a worldview becomes fully Christian when we are willing to bet our lives on this confession:

1. Boulding, *The Meaning of the Twentieth Century*, 163.
2. McKenna, *Megatruth*, 65–88.

>All *history* is interpreted in the Incarnation of Jesus Christ;
>All *humanity* is judged by the Cross of Jesus Christ, and
>All *hope* is found in the Resurrection of Jesus Christ.

As fundamental as these truths may seem, they are the highest order of integration in the teaching and learning process of Christian higher education. While far from complete, they offer a framework not just for scholarly debate, but for practical application in the classroom and realistic assessment of educational outcomes.

EDUCATION AND EVANGELISM

The only new initiative that we took on during our interim year as Executive Director of the CCC involved the World Congress on Evangelization at Lausanne, Switzerland. As an invited delegate, I asked Leighton Ford, Chair of the Lausanne Committee, if we could convene a session on Christian higher education at the Congress. His first response was negative because he did not want to shift attention away from the primary focus of evangelization or create a precedent for other ministries to have special sessions. After we argued that the Great Commission was a seamless document mandating a complementary relationship between evangelism and education and assuring Leighton that our agenda would be limited to that question, he granted us time and place for our session. On behalf of the CCC, Christian educators from around the world were invited to come together to discuss the subject "World Evangelization and Christian Higher Education: Strategy for the Future" and propose a resolution for concerted action.

My keynote address filled out the theme by putting the Great Commission into a unified systems theory in which world evangelization and higher education are inseparable. Gently, but firmly, the challenge was presented:

>Like C. P. Snow's "Two Cultures" of art and science . . . Christian higher education and world evangelization tip their hats, but do not speak . . . They tend to divide into narrow, competing specialties rather than complementary tasks in the kingdom of God. Worst of all, they each seek to multiply by using duplicated resources of men, money, space and time. To me, the two cultures of Christian higher education and evangelism point out a major

issue in world evangelization to which this Congress should address itself.[3]

This challenge set up the main body of the address under the subtitle, "The Great Commission: A World System." Beginning with the sentence, "Christ gave us a 'world view' in the final charge to His disciples," the exposition of the Great Commission results in "an integrated system, flawless in design, world wide in scope, and timeless in application." Within Christ's mandate, then, the essential components for an integrated system were identified as purpose, resources, process, strategy, and objective. This led to the section on "Christian Higher Education and Evangelism" as two working parts of the same system with common and complementary relationships. In common, the two ministries find purpose, power, and objective. In complement, they have their own method and strategy. The conclusion of this section reads:

> Christian higher education should touch each piece of the world evangelization network. At Jerusalem, it becomes a stabilizing force for the moral values that Christianity brings to a culture. In Judea, it is a moral tracking system as the culture grows and changes. In Samaria, it has the openness to explore new options across cultures. For the ends of the earth, Christian higher education has institutions spotted around the globe like stepping stones to the uttermost parts. Also, their institutions house the flesh and fire of the young upon whom world evangelization ultimately depends.[4]

The keynote address ends with a call for "A Plan of Action." First, there is the call for *organic cooperation* in the Lausanne declaration of commitment to the Christian world system. Second, there is the call for *operational collaboration* as evangelists and educators sit down together and ask how they can work together to make "whole men" through "whole systems." Third, in the boldest call of all, there is the proposal for *resource coordination*.

> Following the pattern of the Christian College Consoritum in the United States, it is feasible to envision a worldwide network of educational institutions pledged to the Christian world system. The resources that they would bring to the system could be traced by a computerized directory listing location, programs, people,

3. McKenna, "World Evangelization and Christian Higher Education: Strategy for the Future," 2.

4. Ibid., 13.

and facilities. This could save some of the duplicated costs that are incurred when we assume that we must build new facilities at strategic spots across the world either to extend the Gospel or protect the developmental process with our converts.

In similar vein, we need resource coordination on a worldwide basis of Christian scholars who can give invaluable support to evangelization. A worldwide talent bank of Christian scholars could be developed by a computerized directory that would make it possible to identify some of the most powerful minds in the academic world. As members of an "invisible Christian university" they might correspond, meet for fellowship, speak together on Christian ethics, teach the doctrines of Christ and supportive disciplines, break down the artificial barriers between education and evangelism, and challenge secular scholarship.[5]

Fourth and finally, Christian educators and evangelists were called to come together in *spiritual unity* around the "Wait" and "Go" decisions of Christ's world system.

We are apt to forget the many of the great spiritual awakenings in the world have been ignited by youth on the campus . . . Therefore, rather than educators assuming that evangelism is "not their bag" or taking the stance that "if it comes, it comes," they should be leaders in making "Wait" and "Go" decisions a part of living and learning on the campus. Evangelists, rather than assuming that they are wilderness voices for "Wait" and "Go" decisions or that their task is limited to "making disciples," should consider the campus as the ignition system for the Great Commission.[6]

While the report of the Commission on Christian Higher Education did not become a part of the celebrated Lausanne Covenant, it represented the integration of faith and learning in a new or neglected dimension. Christian scholars from across the world found themselves meeting each other, talking together, and pledging to pray together after returning home. The division between evangelism and education took on new meaning when we met scholars from behind the Iron Curtain who risked their careers and perhaps their lives because they were so hungry for fellowship with other Christian scholars. Sensitivities were also sharpened by the comparison of educational resources in North American colleges and universities and their counterparts in developing countries. Together, in the final session,

5. Ibid., 16–17.
6. Ibid., 18.

the participants pledged to find a way for partnering across international lines, promoting faculty exchange, and developing media networks for sharing resources. Once again, the call was heard for convening a World Congress on Christian Higher Education, a call whose echo can still be heard forty years later.

CCC PRESIDENCY

Coinciding with the Lausanne meeting in June, 1974 the CCC Board announced the appointment of Dr. Gordon Werkema as our new President/ Executive Director. His responsibility as administrator of the Faculty Development project for the Council for the Advancement of Small Colleges delayed the date for assuming his new office until August, but he brought with him the credentials of academic scholarship and presidential leadership, especially in the area of integrating faith and learning, that more than met the expectations of the rewritten task description. With a vision that embraced the whole of Christian higher education, he set the Christian College Consortium on a new course.

13

Pivot Point

SHORT-TERM AND INTERIM LEADERSHIP for the Consortium in the first three years of operations left long-range questions unanswered. Soon after the election of Dr. Gordon Werkema as President in 1974, his vision for the future included some changes that the CCC Board had to weigh carefully.

CCC LOCATION

From the very beginning, the CCC presidents asked the question, "Where should the permanent headquarters of the Consortium be located?" If all things were equal, strong preference was given to the *academic option* modeled after the plan of Clement and Origen, when they located next to the library at Alexandria in order to engage in debate with secular scholars. The Apostle Paul chose a similar model at Ephesus when he rented a station across from the world-class library to hold his seminars and not far from the stadium where he could preach. Such a plan would also be consistent with the dream of a Christian university presence in an academic stronghold of American higher education. A secular academic setting would be a catalyst for advancing the integration of faith and learning because of the ever-present challenge. Thoughts stretched out to Harvard, Yale, Stanford, and Michigan, but without serious consideration.

What might be called the *evangelical option* also had appeal. Under this plan the CCC would be located at the alleged center for evangelical

Christianity, namely the Chicago area where Wheaton College, *Christianity Today*, Tyndale Publishing House, and the National Association of Evangelicals had headquarters. Links with these organizations offered the possibility of networking through their resources and also attracting donors who shared the vision of cooperation in evangelical Christianity as a potent influence in the secular culture. Extra appeal came with the proximity of Wheaton College, a CCC member, with Trinity International University and North Park College as future prospects in the area. Counter-thoughts, however, quickly prevailed. Right or wrong, negative attitudes were attached to the thought of joining the pilgrimage to "the Evangelical Mecca" and cloistering together at a distance from the academic powerhouses of the University of Chicago and Northwestern University. Furthermore, although CCC presidents acknowledged Wheaton College as the flagship for Christian higher education, they felt as if cooperation meant parity in a nationwide network.

Washington DC represented the *political option* as the potential home for the CCC. Although it lacked the identity as an academic or evangelical center, there was never any doubt that our nation's capital stood at the center of political power and national exposure. When Dr. Werkema was elected President of the CCC, he brought with him a strong case for a move to Washington. Having served there as a Vice-President for the Council for the Advancement of Small Colleges and having developed relationships with Christian leaders in the area, he foresaw the advantages of having a physical presence in the Capitol, especially when political winds were blowing contrary to the independence of the Christian college and university. To establish a beachhead in Washington, DC where Christian higher education would be seen and heard had its own appeal. The option was not without reservations. The seductive sirens of power politics brought with them the temptation to shift the direction of the CCC from the independence of its inner-directed mission to plans and programs in response to other-directed cues from a high-pressure environment.

When the three options were weighed, the scales tipped to Washington, DC. The advantages of the location matched the scope of Dr. Werkema's vision. Like bearding the lion in its den, the Christian College Consortium moved into position to increase the visibility of Christian higher education, assure its presence at the center of power, attract interest in cooperative programs, and affirm its distinction in the highest educational councils of the land.

DEFINITION OF INTEGRATION

The integration of faith and learning is not new. Christian scholars have no trouble finding its beginning in the theological premise, "All truth is God's truth" and its centering in the person of Christ, "in whom all things hold together." From then on, the concept runs like a golden thread through the thinking of patriarchs, philosophers, prophets, and preachers from ancient to modern times. When applied to the academic enterprise, the emphasis is heavily weighted toward the intellectual or cognitive component of the human taxonomy. In definitions of the liberal arts in particular, ideas such as "thinking critically," "analyzing objectively," and "seeing synoptically" are familiar to us. These same ideas carry over into the Christian liberal arts through the integrative process. Critical, analytic, and synthetic thinking are conceived as qualities of the Christian mind operating through the lens of a Christian worldview.

But is this enough? CCC presidents brought to the table a holistic view of integration in the Christian liberal arts that goes beyond intellectual belief to spiritual being and moral behavior. The ramifications reach deep into the soul of the Christian college and university. If our educational mission is limited to intellectual integration, our curriculum can be confined to the classroom, our teaching does not go beyond theory, and our professors can be hired exclusively for their scholarship. But if we are committed to holistic Christian higher education we must integrate believing, being, and doing in the experiences of our students. The academic curriculum must be reinforced by the co-curricular environment, intellectual search must be complemented by spiritual decisions, theoretical understanding must be applied to moral issues, Godly living must be practiced in a real life setting, and faculty scholars must be models of maturing Christians for whom the Word is illuminated by the Spirit of God.

CCC presidents did not come to a quick and easy decision. If integration of faith and learning in the curriculum and the classroom represents the distinctive character of Christian higher education, should first attention be given to sharpening our academic identity before proceeding to larger issues? With differences in theological traditions over the relative weight of believing, being, and doing, are we in danger of fragmenting the delicate balance that brought the CCC into being? With the strong working relationship developed among CCC presidents and deans in the Faith/Learning Institutes, should we let this program mature before engaging other campus leaders in areas such as student development and spiritual formation? In the end, these questions gave way to the reality that the character of the Christian college or university cannot be segmented into intellectual, spiritual, and social parts. Otherwise, our campuses lose the potency of the classroom, chapel, and campus community working as one toward wholeness in belief, being and behavior. At this critical juncture, the Dean's Council of the CCC led the presidents in giving voice to a holistic view of integration. At their 1974 meeting, the deans laid the plans for the forthcoming Faith/Learning Institute around this decision, "By consensus, the Council agreed to extend the whatever ways possible the faith/learning relationship to the faith/learning/living relationship." Although the CCC presidents did not formally adopt a definition for the integration of faith and learning at this meeting, the summation of their deliberations lends itself to this general understanding:

> Integration is the scholarly process of exploring openly all dimensions of human learning (centered in the liberal arts) from the perspective of biblical revelation (centered in Jesus Christ) in order to think, live and serve Christianly in the contemporary world.

Around the spirit of this understanding, the integration of Christian faith with learning and living as well as serving became the spirit of understanding for the motto on our masthead.

AMERICAN STUDIES PROGRAM

With its heredity in the integration of Christian faith and human learning and its environment in the political climate of Washington, DC, which way would the CCC go? Werkema found a creative way to unite these diverse worlds. As one of his first acts, he proposed the establishment of an American Studies Program in Washington, DC for the specific purpose of demonstrating the integration of faith and learning in a one-semester program for students of CCC colleges who would have hands-on experience in the workings of government and development of public policy. CCC presidents and deans applauded the idea and gave Dr. Werkema the go-ahead to initiate the program.

In another bold move, Werkema convinced Dr. John Bernbaum, who lived and breathed a commitment to the integrative concept, to take a leave of absence from his position at the State Department in order to lead the program. One year later, fifty students from fifteen colleges had participated in the program and given the highest commendation to this unique experience of seeing how their Christian faith related to the opportunities as well as to the problems of public service. The American Studies Program soon became the centerpiece for fulfilling the original purposes of the Consortium and a model for other cooperative programs among the institutions.

RESEARCH ON INTEGRATION

The success of the American Studies Program closed another gap in the integrative process. Applying the scholarly writing in the history, theology, and philosophy of integration in Christian higher education, the ASP proved that the concept could be implemented in a cooperative curriculum bringing Christian faith and political science together. Still, a yawning gap had not been filled. Research studies on the educational outcomes of integration in Christian higher education did not exist. In the original planning session for the CCC in 1971, Dr. Earl McGrath challenged us with the question, "Are evangelical colleges actually having the kind of impact which they profess to have on the development of Christian values and theological perspectives among students?" He then encouraged us to consider the establishment of research programs that would enable the colleges to improve their programs, and at the same time, demonstrate the effectiveness of the claims that they make as Christian liberal arts colleges. McGrath's challenge hung suspended over the claims for the CCC until a five-year, 1.5 million dollar research project was developed by Dr. Werkema and proposed to the Lilly Endowment, under the title, "Evaluating the Outcomes of the Christian Liberal Arts College and Values in Christian Higher Education." The purpose of the study was summed up in three questions:

1. Are Christian colleges succeeding in developing a Christian perspective on learning and life that differs from secular institutions in significant ways?

2. Are Christian college students gaining an understanding of moral issues and social movements through the Christian liberal arts?

3. Are the academic programs and campus climates of Christian colleges reaching their educational goals, not just in cognition, but in the volitional and affective domains as well?[1]

1. Werkema, "Proposal to the CCC Executive Committee," 1976.

In keeping with the standards of research, three phases were projected for the five-year period: Phase I—Design; Phase II—Administration; and Phase III—Reporting and Publication. The CCC Board proposed a research team with David McKenna as Research Director, Earl McGrath as Senior Consultant, a Research Advisory Council of prominent researchers, such as Ted Ward, Merton Strommen, and Ruth Eckert, and a Faculty Researcher from each CCC college as facilitators for the project on the local campus. Regrettably, the project was not funded, but the proposal served the purpose of putting the assessment of educational outcomes related to the integration of faith, learning, and living high on the agenda for the future.

COUNCIL OR COALITION

Along with the move to Washington, DC and the development of the American Studies Program, Gordon Werkema's ambitious agenda for the future of the Consortium included his proposal for the establishment of the Christian College Coalition with membership for "those interested in religiously integrated values in higher education." A significant change is evident in these words. Consortium membership was determined by demonstrated leadership in the integration of faith and learning, while Coalition membership was open by declaration of interest in the process. This change is readily seen in the goals for the Coalition that were primarily political in purpose: (a) monitoring of legislation, judicial activity, and public opinion on matters which could affect the freedom of Christian colleges to function educationally and religiously; (b) development of unified positions on critical issues for presentation to other organizations, governmental bodies, and public policy formers; and (c) development of an offensive position on potential erosions of religious and educational freedom in the Christian college movement.

The opening invitation produced a few responses, but when the suspicions fell, the impulse picked up momentum and membership began to grow exponentially. At first, the Consortium and the Coalition danced as awkward partners, but before long, it was apparent that the "think tank and pilot" purposes of the Consortium and the associational plans of the Coalition were too diverse for one organization. The residual question was, "To whom would be entrusted the primary responsibility for the integration of faith and learning, living and serving in Christian higher education?" The answer to this question would be a turning point, not just in the history of the Consortium, but in Christian higher education itself.

After careful consideration, the CCC presidents gave strong support for Werkema's proposal and backed up their position with every CCC institution becoming a charter member of the Coalition. The stage was set, however, for increasing tension over the primary purpose of the CCC and control of the expanding organization. Although the Coalition started out as a subsidiary of the Consortium, it soon began to take on a life of its own. With the new members of the Coalition came the latent feelings that the Consortium was an "elitist" organization or a "president's club." Not even the plan for adding five members a year assuaged the critics. Once the tide began to roll, a division between parent and child organizations became inevitable. After Gordon Werkema resigned as President of the Consortium/Coalition in 1977 and John Dellenback, an esteemed Christian layperson with political credentials as a member of Congress, assumed the CCC presidency, the die was cast. Although Dellenback did an astute job of balancing the interests of the Consortium and the Coalition for five years, in 1981 the legal separation was made. Dr. Carl Lundquist, retired President of Bethel College and a charter member of the CCC, was named President of the Consortium with the specific purpose of continuing to be a "think tank" with pilot programs dedicated to the integration of faith and learning. In that context, the Dean's Council made a strong case for keeping oversight of the American Studies Program, but politically-savvy John Dellenback got a grant from friends in Oregon designating 90 percent of the funds to the American Studies Program for use at the discretion of the Coalition Board. From then on, the Coalition claimed programs dedicated to the integration of faith and learning as companions to its political purpose.

Because of my intimate involvement in the founding and early leadership of the Consortium, people often ask how I felt about the separation of the Coalition and its assumption of the American Studies Program. With complete candor, I confess my concerns. Foremost was the question about continuing the emphasis upon the integration of faith and learning, living and serving. Political impact defined the purpose of the Coalition, criteria for membership did not include demonstrated evidence of academic excellence or integrative learning, and John Dellenback offered no formal credentials for leadership of the concept. I feared that political issues would overwhelm quality concerns, open membership would dilute the academic strength of the Coalition, and Dellenback's lack of understanding would shortchange the integrative concept.

I proved to be wrong. Yes, John's personal priorities for leadership were in the political realm with advocacy for the Christian higher education in such cases a Grove City College and Mississippi College, but I failed to recognize the value of his political nose for sensing the needs of his constituency. With deft strokes, he gave John Bernbaum a free hand in developing the American Studies Program, named Rich Gathro as his Executive Vice-President and hired Karen Longman to lead in renewing the curriculum, developing the faculty, and assessing the outcomes for the integration of faith, learning, living, and serving. I fully agree with Dan Chamberlain's assessment of Dellenback's leadership at the time of his retirement when he said that the Coalition goes forward with "vitality, visbility, and viability."

Meanwhile, the Christian College Consortium went through the process of changing leadership, location and focus. Dr. Carl Lundquist, retired President of Bethel College and senior statesman in the evangelical world, accepted the part-time position as President of the CCC and moved its offices to his home base in St. Paul, Minnesota. Although the American Studies Program has been shifted to the Coalition, Lundquist's stature in Christian higher education and his passionate commitment to the integration of faith and learning kept the concept alive among the CCC presidents. As witness to this continuing interest, significant grants from the Pew Charitable Trust in the later 1980s kept the Consortium on the front edge of interdisciplinary studies and faculty development in the humanities. Carl Lundquist, like his colleague John Dellenback, brought the gift of community to his professional as well as personal relationships. Annual meetings of the CCC became prized moments for presidents and spouses to come together for mutual learning from the experiences of leadership along with in-depth discussions of relevant issues in Christian higher education. Major endowment funds also came to the CCC during Dr. Lundquist's tenure, including the Vechery Scholarship fund, shepherded by future CCC President Tom Englund, to assist needy students with Christian leadership skills to attend CCC colleges.

Even though the CCC stepped aside to let the CCCU take center stage, the perspective of history confirms its founding purpose and its pivotal position as a turning point in Christ-centered higher education. In support of its continuing mission, the CCC website puts its history into the capsule:

Marshalling its resources in cooperative efforts, the CCC assisted in the development of programs for both faculty and students, as well as the educational philosophy that came to be known as 'the integration of faith and learning.' In 1976, it established the Christian College Coalition; a sister institution, now known as the Council for Christian Colleges & Universities, and serving over 111 institutions in North America as well as affiliate schools around the world.[2]

Most important, however, is the word of the historian, William Ringenberg, who writes, "the organization of the Christian College Consortium in 1971 represented one of the more noteworthy efforts to facilitate the reconstruction of Christian higher education in America."[3]

2. Gordon Werkema, grant proposal to the Lilly Endowment, "Evaluating the Outcomes of the Christian Liberal Arts College and Values in Higher Education."

3. Ibid.

14

Transformational Traction

A TAINT OF "ELITISM" dogs the history of the Christian College Consortium. With the announcement in 1971 that eleven Christian colleges had come together to advance the cause and champion the distinctive of Christian higher education, others immediately wanted to join. Not even the explanation that the Lilly grant for the venture limited the original number or that plans called for an addition of five new members per year sufficed. Dissatisfaction rumbled underground until its surfaced with the charge of "elitism" and the label of a "president's club." Once the judgment was made, it tended to stick. As one of the founding presidents and first Chair of the Christian College Consortium (CCC), even current presidents have let me know that the perception has been passed down from generation to generation. The fact that the Consortium has continued to hold an annual meeting of presidents and spouses since its separation from the Coalition probably reinforces the elitist perception.

A TRANSFORMATIONAL MODEL

Whenever I tried to dispel the charge of elitism to critics, I felt a defensive edge. Then I read James Davison Hunter's book, *To Change the World: The Irony, Tragedy and Possibility of Christianity in the Late Modern World*. His premise is that evangelical Christians have failed to change our culture because we have chosen the wrong tactics.[1] Rational idealism, individual conversion, spiritual revival, popular marketing, and power politics have all failed. To paraphrase Hunter's alternative,

> Transformational change comes through elitist leaders from credible institutions who are near the center of power and network together around a commanding truth to develop cooperative programs and exercise faithful presence to alter the fabric of the prevailing culture.[2]

Without force-fitting the CCC into Hunter's model, each of the components for transformation comes to life in its history. Of course, Hunter's model had not been conceived at the time of the founding of the CCC. Whether inspiration, intuition, or propitious timing accounts for the similarity between the Hunter model and the history of the CCC, we make no claim. Perhaps the best answer is, "All of the above." Readers are invited to pass their own judgment on the following similarities.

ELITIST LEADERS

Yes, the first CCC presidents were elitist, but not because they were condescending, exclusive and controlling. In his model, Hunter redeems the word "elitist" to mean a group of leaders who are come from credible institutions and, even though out on the periphery of the culture, they are close enough to the center of power to affect a measure of transformational change.[3] If the resources of the Lilly grant had permitted, more Christian college presidents would have been selected. The fundable number of thirteen to fifteen presidents made it necessary to select persons who were recognized in higher education as advocates for academic excellence and represented regional Christian liberal arts colleges of reputation among their peers. Although the presidents and their institutions did not have the prestige attributed to those at the center of power in higher education, they were close enough to affect change in the culture.

---

1. Hunter, *To Change the World*, 32.
2. Ibid., 255–72.
3. Ibid., 42–43.

CREDIBLE INSTITUTIONS

Credible institutions meant more than reputation in the academic community. The schools that were selected also had to have resources beyond regular operations to invest in CCC membership and cooperative programs. Endowments varied and many operated on the narrow margins of a balance of enrollment numbers, tuition revenues, and student financial aid. Boards and presidents had to share the vision for the Consortium to make a difference in Christian higher education as well as for their own institutions.

COMMANDING TRUTH

The commitment to what Hunter called a "commanding truth" gave the Consortium its common cause, its cohesive force, and its impetus for action.[4] High on the agenda was the motivation for the institutions to "do together what they could not do by themselves," but this came in a distant second to the drive to advance the integration of faith and learning as the quality that defines the character of the Christian college and identifies its contribution to the dialogue in higher education. For many Christian colleges and universities, the integration of faith and learning was a shibboleth for marketing, but not a cohesive and energizing center fully embraced by the board, president, academic deans, and faculty. Presidents who came to Phoenix for the planning meeting of the CCC in 1971 brought with them the assurance that every unit of leadership within their institution—board, president, deans, and faculty—gave full support to the integrative concept. Especially, they came with evidence of integration implemented in the curriculum and faculty development. Again, this is not to say that other institutions were failing at this point, but only accentuates the centrality of the concept in the total selection process. For good reason, we named the integration of faith and learning the "soul" of a Christian college.

4. Ibid., 32.

INSTITUTIONAL NETWORKS

Even though we had not yet heard about the potency of James Davison Hunter's overlapping institutional networks,[5] the germ of the idea came to fruition in the organization of the CCC. With the intent of laying the groundwork for a future national network, the charter colleges were chosen from five regions—East Coast, North Central, Midwest, South, and West. Projecting forward, regional members had the privilege of recommending a new member from their respective area. George Fox College and Trinity Evangelical College soon came to membership by regional nomination. Presidents also brought overlapping networks with them. Four of the presidents, for instance, had served as President of the National Association of Evangelicals. Leaders of denominational colleges added national and international networks of their own. Most, if not all, of the presidents had personal connections with the Prayer Breakfast Movement, the World Congress on Evangelization, the World Evangelical Fellowship, held membership in the Council for the Advancement of Small Colleges (renamed the Council for Independent Colleges in 1956), and participated selectively in the meetings of such educational associations as the Association of American Colleges (AAC), American Council on Education (ACE), Association of Governing Boards (AGB), and later, the National Association for Independent Colleges and Universities (NAICU), and the Council for Advancement of Service to Education (CASE). Perhaps most important of all is the fact that in the Body of Christ, there are only two or three degrees of separation between its members. When Christian believers meet and give the names and affiliations of those they know, the networking bond is almost instantaneous. The potency of these overlapping institutional networks proved to be the silent source of strength for both the Consortium and the Coalition.

FAITHFUL PRESENCE

The Consortium was not founded to storm the gates of a pagan academic community or a secular society. Rather, to capture the spirit that runs like a thread through Hunter's book, CCC and its leadership exercised the "faithful presence" of being gatekeepers of the integrative concept for Christian higher education and credible witnesses for academic excellence, freedom

5. Ibid., 37–38.

and integrity in all of American higher education.[6] The reception by presidents of secular colleges and universities, both public and private, was surprising. After completing my term as Chair of the Consortium board, I ventured into the stuffy world of the Association of American Colleges, taking my identity as president of an evangelical Christian college with me to membership on the Board of Directors. About that time, the National Association of Independent Colleges was formed and I was nominated for the board as a representative of evangelical Christian higher education. When officers were elected, they asked me to serve as Secretary. Out of that position, I became a member of what might be called an "Odd Triplet." The President of Brigham Young University, Dallin Oaks, the Provost of the University of Notre Dame, James Burtchaell, and I worked together to persuade the Equal Employment Opportunities Commission to permit independent, church-related colleges and universities to exempt "creed" from their equal opportunities statement for employment of faculty and staff.

From then on, one thing led to another. With strong convictions about self-regulation as the buffer against the intrusion of state and federal authority, I served as a member of the Council on Post-secondary Accreditation as well as the Council of Presidents for the American Council on Education. When President Jimmy Carter paid a campaign promise to teacher's unions and proposed the establishment of the Department of Education with a seat on the President's Cabinet, I became an opposition voice. With firm conviction that education belonged to the states, I took a public stand against a federal agency with the money and the bureaucracy to control and regulate education at all levels and in all sectors. While Christian higher education was my primary concern, my experience as a principal of a Christian academy and a professor at Michigan and Ohio State led me to advocacy for public sectors as well.

All of this led to the surprise call from Senator Mark Hatfield asking if he could nominate me as Secretary of Education in the Reagan Cabinet. When I accepted the nomination and asked him what I should do, he answered, "If God is in it, it will be." Later, after learning that the process for political appointments is as messy as making sausage or passing legislation, I realized that the appointment would have been a disaster. Even Terrel Bell, who beat out a couple of us for the position, ended up in President Reagan's disfavor because he failed to fulfill his charge to eliminate the Department of Education. "If God is in it, it will be" has the corollary, "If God is not in it,

6. Ibid., 95–96.

it will not be." That disappointment led me to give the greatest speech of my life when I returned from Washington to tell the students at Seattle Pacific University, "I would rather be your President than his Secretary." Still, out of my fifteen minutes of fame, the experience confirmed Hunter's proposition that leaders who are on the periphery, but close to the center of power, can have a transforming effect on the culture of which they are a part.

TRANSFORMATIONAL LEADERSHIP

John Dellenback and Bob Andringa, past Presidents of the CCCU, exemplify credible leaders close to the center of power bringing about transformational change. Although neither of them came with executive leadership experience in the Christian college as did Gordon Werkema, Myron Augsburger, and Paul Corts, each of them brought timely credentials to the CCCU to match the need of the moment. John Dellenback came to the presidency of the Consortium/Coaltion from a ranking position as Congressman from the State of Oregon and as Director of the Peace Corps. Bob Andringa had served as Minority Staff Director of the House Committee on Education for Al Quie, the congressman from Minnesota and ranking members of the Committee, before assuming the position as Executive Director of the Education Commission of the States. In each case, we recognized the credentials of effective leadership close to the center of political and educational power in Washington. More than that, they had cultivated overlapping networks that touched on every phase of politics, education, and religion in the nation's capitol. With that extensive background, they had leverage for change that Christian higher education had never before known. While the phenomenal growth of the CCCU is one witness to their effectiveness, the drama of transformation from the 1950s when Christian colleges were a fragmented, peripheral and defensive sector to the current era of significance came when Robert Andringa, President of the CCCU, was invited to a seat as an equal and respected partner in the Washington Higher Education Secretariat, a forum dedicated "to consider strategic issues, to review trends/challenges confronting higher education, and to develop responses and to learn from colleagues and external experts."[7]A far cry from the time when Christian colleges and universities were condemned to be as "extinct as the whooping crane."

7. Washington Higher Education Secretariat, website.

A PERSPECTIVE ON HISTORY

What perspective on the history of the Christian College Consortium can we draw from these observations? If Hunter's model for transformational change is applied to Consortium history, step by step, one could argue that the CCCU would not have come into existence without the CCC. All prior attempts to create a national association for Christian higher education had failed because of fragmentation, isolation, and defensive attitudes. Despite complaints about the elitism of the Consortium, initial invitations to the Coalition resulted in a weak response. Only John Dellenback's aggressive recruiting brought Coalition membership to its "critical mass." As we have already seen, he too carried the label of an elitist with overlapping networks who was located close to the center of power and motivated by commanding truth.

A counter argument might contend that the Born Again movement in 1976 would have brought the Coalition into being as a grass roots organization without the influence of the CCC. If so, according to Hunter, it would remain weak and ineffective because "Even where the impetus for changes draws from popular agitation, it does not gain traction until it is embraced by elites."[8] This may explain why earlier calls for national and world congresses on Christian higher education failed. Before the Consortium, there were no credible elites with overlapping networks ready embrace and propagate these "bottom up" or "grass roots" ventures.

Returning to Hunter's transformational thesis, we see the Consortium in the vital role as the forerunner in a transformational movement leading to the CCCU as a formidable force close to the center of power in American higher education. True to the role of a forerunner, the CCC: (a) embraced the commanding truth of the integration of faith and learning; (b) organized presidential leaders with overlapping networks to advance the concept; (c) foresaw the broader need for an association of Christian colleges and universities; (d) approved the formation of the Coalition, gave it early leadership, recognized the commonality of its founding purpose; and (e) set the Coalition free to grow on its own into a full service organization involving theorists who conceive ideas, researchers who test the ideas, teachers who communicate the ideas, and practitioners who apply the ideas at grass roots levels.

8. Hunter, *To Change the World*, 41.

From this perspective, we come back full cycle to conclude that transformational change in the culture of Christian higher education could not have taken place without the CCC as the forerunner and the CCCU as its proud progeny. Through the tread of the CCC, the CCCU found its traction.

15

Energizing Impulse

ARE WE WITNESSES TO the rebirth of Christian higher education in the past fifty years? If so, is Christian higher education a movement with the momentum to carry it to a new level of significance in the future? It is time to pause, answer these questions, and determine whether or not we can justify the title of this book, *Christ-centered Higher Education: Memory, Meaning and Momentum for the 21st Century.*

Mark Noll gives us a guide for our writing in his book, *Turning Points: Decisive Moments in the History of Christianity.* After retracing twelve events in Christian history, such as the Council of Nicea and the coronation of Charlemagne, Noll poses three questions to determine whether or not an event qualifies as a historical turning point.

1. Why was this event crucial?

2. How did it relate to what went before and lead to what followed?

3. What might those of us looking at the end of the twentieth century [or, we might add, the beginning of the twenty-first century] learn from the event?[1]

While not pretending that the happenings in Christian higher education in the twentieth century are as momentous as those cited by Noll throughout Christian history, we can ask these same questions of this era and let the answers speak for themselves.

1. Noll, *Turning Points*, 14.

PROPITIOUS TIMING

As with all events that qualify as turning points, timing is everything. In the case of the CCC, its founding in 1971 came a time when two external forces were converging to create a critical intersection for Christian higher education. First, *American higher education had failed as the Savior of the society.* The unbridled hope that higher education had promised for social transformation after World War II was dashed to the ground by the violence of student protest on the campuses of the nation, including the Kent State killings in 1970. Second, *evangelical Christianity showed the first signs of spiritual awakening with clout in the public sphere.* 1976 is marked as the Year of the Evangelical and the rise of the Born Again movement. In this climate of cataclysmic change, Christian higher education was at a turning point. Would we triumphantly point out the fact that our students were not trashing the president's office and threatening to bomb corporate buildings? Would we gloat "I told you so" over the corpse of secular idealism?

The CCC chose neither option. If any claim to the founding of the CCC as a crucial event can be made, it is in same kind of response that the Bobby Kennedy made when he was pushed to declare American democracy as the counterforce to Soviet communism. Kennedy said, "It is what we are for, not what we are against."

The CCC was founded under the aegis of integrating of biblical revelation and human reason as the distinctive characteristic that defines what Christian higher education stands for, not what it stands against. In this affirmation, the meaning and the spirit of the Christian college was reborn. Like Paul's declaration to the Greeks in the Areopagus, there was no condemnation of the many gods whom they worshipped, but rather a transcending vision into the character of the God whom they sought. The founding of the CCC qualifies as an "Athens moment" because it lifts the character of Christ-centered college and university to a level of distinction that no other institution of higher education can match. Since then, integration has been the yeast in the loaf of both the CCC and the CCCU. Let this witness stand as sufficient testimony of a crucial and significant event.

HISTORICAL CONTINUITY

The drama of rebirth can be readily seen in the comparative status of Christian higher education in middle decade of the twentieth century and the second decade of the twenty-first century. In these changes, we see the signs of renaissance that should be recorded in the history of American higher education with as much objectivity as the defection from the faith among Christian colleges in the nineteenth century.

From endangered species to robust body. Witnesses to the present status of Christian colleges and universities would find it hard to believe that the sector was predicted to become as "extinct as the whooping crane" in mid-twentieth century. Whereas the growth of the public sector was expected to undercut Christian colleges and speed their demise, enrollment in the sector throughout the last two decades of the twentieth century outdistanced all comers, including fast-rising community colleges. While some might raise the question that growth came at the expense of quality, especially in the expansion of professional, graduate, degree completion, and online programs, there is sufficient evidence that on-campus, undergraduate enrollments more than held their own. Although the total number of students in Christian colleges and universities continues to be miniscule in comparison with the public sector, their surprising growth against dire predictions is a phenomenon in itself.

From splintered weakness to cooperative strength. The founding of the CCC marked the first time that diverse Christian colleges put aside their differences in order to cooperate. Fragmentation without hostility characterized the relationship of such diverse colleges as Wheaton, Seattle Pacific, Messiah, and Bethel. Differences in theology, educational philosophy, admissions standards, and behavioral expectations kept tipping their hats, but never really walking arm in arm. But, with the establishment of the CCC, leaders of diverse institutions saw their common goal and agreed to a student exchange program for dependent children of their respective faculties. Some CCC members had reservations about schools that admitted non-Christians or held a more liberal behavioral code, but even these differences did not deter the spirit of cooperation that brought the group together. Without serious dissent, the CCC members moved forward together. Even more important, the founding of the CCC demonstrated the power of concerted action. Individual institutions had relative strength in their regions of the country, but until the national network of the CCC was formed, Christian higher education had no national voice. The decision to invite regional prospects for membership opened the door to the future network of CCCU memberships that would literally embrace the nation. Suddenly, the strength of numbers, especially significant numbers, became apparent. The CCCU could exercise an influence that could change Christian higher education.

From voiceless minority to effective advocate. In the 1950s, Christian higher education suffered, not just from being demeaned in the centers of academic power, but from the lack of a common voice through which it could make itself heard even in the evangelical Christian community. Attempts to bring Christian colleges and universities together under the umbrella of the National Association of Evangelicals or other agencies failed and failed miserably. Christian liberal arts colleges, Bible colleges, and evangelical seminaries went their separate ways. Even among colleges of the same denomination, a competitive spirit muffled any attempts at a unified voice. Sixty years later, the CCCU is an international coalition of 113 members in North America and 72 affiliate institutions in 25 countries with a respected voice in the highest councils of American higher education. Even more dramatically, the beleaguered sector of the 1950s lacked any standing in the associations that represented American higher education. In the educational councils of Washington, DC, for instance, Christian higher education was ignored, if not demeaned. At best, Christian college presidents joined the Council for the Advancement of Small Colleges (later Council of Independent Colleges) and participated in the early meetings of the National Association of Independent Colleges and Universities (NAICU), but neither of those national associations gave Christian higher education its own voice. With the founding of the CCC, we who were presidents of Christian colleges worked our way individually into positions on such boards as the NAICU, CIC, and the Association of American Colleges. Once the Christian College Coalition was created as an arm of the Consortium in Washington, DC, however, evangelical Christian higher education found its unified voice and showed its cooperative strength. Today, the CCCU has its place at the table of the Washington Secretariat with fifty other associations of higher education, its presidents frequently hold board positions in the NAICU and CIC, and when political or legal issues affecting Christian higher education are raised, its chief executive is never bypassed.

From defensive posture to optimistic attitude. How often can you be told that you are doomed to die, demeaned as irrelevant, or destined to become extinct without becoming a little paranoid? No wonder that so many Christian colleges in the 1950s and 1960s hunkered down behind the posture of a beleaguered minority suffering for the truth and striking back against the evils of public higher education. It created the vicious cycle of a self-fulfilling prophecy that, at one and the same time, lowered the self-esteem of Christian higher education while raising its defenses. Perhaps the most dramatic evidence of rebirth came when that vicious cycle was broken and the self-esteem of Christian higher education gained self-confidence by the affirmation of its Christ-centered purpose and its show of cooperative strength. With heads high and spirits soaring, Christian colleges and universities walked hand in hand into the twenty-first century with their own story of being "Born Again."

A WORD OF CAUTION

Christian higher education came into the 21st century riding the crest of success. The threat of extinction from external forces, such as declining enrollments and diminishing economics, has temporarily disappeared. Success, however, carries its own threat. Under the assumption that prosperity is a perpetual promise, Christian colleges and universities can be lulled into short-term decisions without considering long-term consequences. Crusty old Warren Buffett had it right when he warned against the false optimism of economic prosperity by saying, "You don't know who's swimming naked until the tide goes out."[2] Past history, however, suggests that Christian colleges and universities are particularly adept at surviving through economic downturns.

The greater threat to the future may be a subtle pattern of cultural change similar to the one that George Marsden describes in his book, *The Soul of the American University: From Protestant Establishment to Established Nonbelief.* As the subtitle implies, American colleges and universities, even public institutions, departed from an era in the nineteenth century when religion was an integral part of the curriculum and the campus. This position was supported by a symbiotic relationship between sectarian higher education and the established Protestant culture. When urbanization, immigration, and industrialization eroded the hegemony of the Protestant culture, the support system for religion in higher education was weakened and the institutions became vulnerable to the intellectual inroads of scientific naturalism. Marsden concludes, "In the nineteenth century Protestant establishment became informal and declared itself nonsectarian. Today, nonsectarianism has come to mean the exclusion

2. Warren Buffett, "Oracle of Omaha," online.

of all religious concerns. In effect, only purely naturalistic viewpoints are allowed a serious academic hearing."[3]

Marsden does not see the same pattern among evangelical Christian colleges because many were founded, not under the umbrella of the Protestant establishment, but in reaction to religious fundamentalism, especially in the first sixty years of the twentieth century. His case holds until the 1970s when the evangelical Christian subculture rose to power and prominence along with the rebirth of the Christian college sector. The question is, "If the evangelical Christian subculture wanes in the 21st century like the Protestant establishment in the 20th century, will evangelical Christ-centered colleges and universities retain their integrity or become vulnerable, not to scientific naturalism, but to secular humanism?" Out of the history of the CCC and the CCCU come three strengths that can sustain the Christ-centered college and university even if the popularity and power of the evangelical Christian subculture passes.

A COMMANDING TRUTH

Christian higher education came to an intersection in the mid-1960s, when we shifted from being "faith-defending" to "faith-affirming" institutions by reclaiming our purpose in the axiom, "All truth is God's truth." The sweep of all creation rings in these words and our confidence rises as we weigh the implications for teaching and learning in the Christian liberal arts. But, we also need the corollary truth that gave the CCC its incentive for action. "All things hold together in Jesus Christ" is the cohesive force behind the integration of faith and learning that goes hand in hand with the creative word, "All truth is God's truth." Together, they give momentum to the movement of Christian higher education that will continue to energize the future.

A PROVEN PROCESS

Reaching all of the way back to the Jesus' response to the Greeks and Paul's sermon at the Aeropagus, the question, "What Jerusalem to do with Athens?" has been asked in each new generation. It will still be the question of tomorrow for Christian scholars and their students. Biblical revelation will still be the final, inspired, and infallible Word of God as human knowledge

3. Marsden, *The Soul of the American University*, 440

fluctuates under change and advances toward truth. Illumination by the God-breathed Spirit will still be the catalyst that unites sound learning and vital piety. Although the approach to integration will vary by discipline and method, the search will still be summed up in the questions, "Where do revelation and reason concur?" "Where do they conflict?" and "What are the imponderables calling for further research?" If committed Christian scholars openly explore and honestly answer these questions, the momentum for movement of Christian higher education that we have seen in the last 40 years will be sustained.

A DIFFERENTIATING IDENTITY

As we have already seen, the self-image of Christian colleges and universities underwent a radical make-over in the mid-1960s with the decision to be known as "faith-affirming" rather than "faith-defending" institutions. The new designation had a transforming influence on the outlook of leadership in Christian higher education. In the midst of the dark days of assassinations, controversial warfare, urban turmoil, and student protest, Christian higher education sounded a note of hope that became a watchword for the rising evangelical movement. Rather than wallowing in defensive warfare with fundamentalists or liberals, the new evangelicals took their name literally and began communicating the "Good News" of an affirming faith. Fifty years later, the term of "faith-based" organizations still carries a positive note in the public mind and in political circles. But then, the history of American higher education comes back to remind us that generic terms open the door for interpretations that can lead to defections from the faith. "Faith-affirming" is equally vulnerable to the widest range of interpretations, from decidedly Christian to decidedly Islamic. When the Christian College Consortium was organized in 1971, the presidents accepted both the "faith-affirming" and "evangelical" designations for their identity, but then became very specific in their commitment to the integration of biblical faith and human learning. Christ alone became the center stake in the conviction that "All things hold together in him." So, the identity of the "Christ-centered" college and university was reborn with the organization of the CCC and the CCCU. It is a bold claim that not only differentiates "Christ-centered" colleges and universities from their secular peers, but also challenges schools in the broad realm of Christian higher education to declare their colors. Even more specifically, "Christ-centered" is a claim that disciplines every facet of academic life and holds the leadership accountable for its outcomes. Yet, it is the differentiation of this identity that fuels Christian higher education as a movement from generation to generation. Members of the CCC and its progeny in the CCCU must declare without apology their "Christ-centered" identity to assure momentum for the movement.

TRAJECTORY INTO TOMORROW

With the dynamic strength of a commanding truth, a sustaining process, and differentiating identity, where will this lead us? Again, in the life cycle of organizations, decline will be inevitable unless there is a breakout vision that is a catalyst taking the movement to the next level of its potential. At present, the Council for Christian Colleges and Universities is the vehicle entrusted with the primary responsibility for advancing the integration of faith and learning in the general sector of Christian higher education. To envision a new thrust for the movement is not a criticism of the CCCU. What the CCCU does, it does well and should keep on doing it, especially in resourcing the advancement of integration in the teaching-learning processes at all levels of institutional development. I have no formal authority to project the future of the CCCU. This is the role of its board and its presidential leadership. But, as a longtime observer and impassioned advocate for Christ-centered higher education, I have a dream. So, in the spirit of a lifetime love, permit me to trace the trajectory of momentum that can take the integration of faith and learning to the next level of impact and penetration in global as well as American higher education.

PART 4

Sustaining Momentum

"A movement is sustained by the vision of commanding truth advancing into new space with greater impact at a higher level."

16

Vision Revisited

QUAKERS GREET EACH OTHER with the question, "How does the truth prosper in thy parts?" With the confession that "Jesus is Lord" as the commanding truth for the integration of faith and learning in the Christ-centered college and university, our presidents might well meet and greet each other with the query, "How does the truth prosper in thy parts?"

Forty years have passed since the founding the Christian College Consortium. During this time, sixty-two persons have served under full time appointment as presidents of the thirteen institutions with an average tenure of eight years. In recognition of these leaders, a roster of CCC presidents from 1971 to 2011 is included as an appendix to this book. A quick scan of the names tells another story in itself, a story of Christian leaders with wide influence in the church, education and society who, under the call of God, preserved and advanced the mission of the Christ-centered college or university in their generation. With this stability of leadership comes a strength that reinforces the commanding truth, sustaining process and differentiating identity that undergirds the integration of faith and learning. Who better to ask the Quaker question, "How does the truth prosper in these parts?" than these faithful colleagues?

PRESIDENTIAL SURVEY

Has the Christian College Consortium fulfilled its purpose of advancing the integration of faith and learning on member campuses, in Christian higher education, and in the larger academic community? In July 2011, thirty-eight CCC presidents, past and present, were invited to complete a survey around that question. For the purposes of the survey, integration was defined as:

> The scholarly process of exploring openly all dimensions of human learning (centered in the liberal arts) from the perspective of biblical revelation (centered in the Person of Jesus Christ) in order to think, live and serve Christianly in the contemporary world.

Twenty-nine (76 percent) of the presidents responded with the understanding that their answers were confidential and would not be used to make comparisons among CCC or non-CCC schools. Because of the size of the sample, only mean scores plus inspection of variations among the answers are used in the following summary of results. The purpose is not to draw complex statistical comparisons, but to gather perceptions, identify trends and project needs. For each question, the presidents were asked to rate the strength of the integrative concept on a five-point scale ranging from 1 being "Very Weak" to 5 being "Very Strong."

INTEGRATION IN ACADEMIC DEVELOPMENT

A. *Curricular Planning and Reform: How would you rate the strength of the integrative concept on curricular planning and implementation during the time of your administration?*

	Mean Score
Student Development	4.46
Chapel	4.43
Core Curriculum	4.39
Athletics	4.08
Professional Majors	4.07
International Studies	4.05
Graduate Studies	3.90
Extension	3.85
Online Learning	3.43

According to the presidents' responses, chapel, student development, and the core Christian liberal arts curriculum comprise the center of the soul of the Christian college or university. The farther we get from the center with curricular or co-curricular programs, the weaker the influence of the integrative concept. Upward extensions into graduate studies and outward extensions into international and urban programs, degree completion and enrichment studies, and new delivery systems, such as online learning, pose a current and future challenge for the integration of faith and learning.

B. *Instructional Methods: How would you rate the strength of the integrative process in faculty scholarship and teaching during the time of your administration?*

	Mean Score
Faculty understanding of the history, theology, and philosophy of integration	4.10
Faculty disciplinary teaching for integration	3.86
Faculty implementation of integrationin course planning	3.79
Faculty research and publication on integration	3.69
Faculty interdisciplinary teaching on integration	3.75
Faculty innovation on integrative teaching	3.59

The presidents' responses show the strength of faculty understanding of the history, theology, and philosophy of integration. The high rating confirms the number and quality of scholarly resources that are available around the subject. Understanding integration then gets translated into course planning and classroom teaching in the faculty members' disciplines. While the strength of integration continues in faculty research, interdisciplinary teaching and innovative instructional methods, there is wide variation among the responses in these areas.

C. *Faculty Development: How would you rate the strength of integrative influence upon faculty development during the time of your tenure?*

	Mean Score:
Recruitment of faculty	4.46

Tenure of faculty	4.38
Orientation of faculty	4.17
Promotion of faculty	4.14
Nurturing of faculty	3.93
Grants and awards	3.39

CCC colleges give strong emphasis to integration in recruiting, tenuring, promoting, and orienting faculty, but less attention to mentoring, nurturing, and rewarding faculty. Does this finding tend to confirm the concern that new faculty, after being selected for their interest in integration, are then left on their own to develop the concept in their teaching and research? Even though the total mean scores are high for recruiting, orienting, promoting, and tenuring faculty, inspection shows wide variation among the CCC colleges.

D. *Assessment of Student Outcomes: How would you rate the strength of integration in student outcomes during the time of your administration?*

Christian character and lifestyle	4.17
Christian competence in career	3.93
Christian leadership in culture	3.76
Christian worldview	3.83
Christian leadership in church	3.69

Composite scores for the areas of the survey show that the assessment of student outcomes is the weakest link in the integrative process. Still, because assessment of integration is unique to the Christian college and university, the ratings are commendable. The order of the ratings is of particular interest. Does the strength of the outcomes in Christian character and lifestyle for CCC colleges mean that our graduates are exceptions to the polls showing that Christians are not much different in these areas than their secular peers? Does the lesser strength of the outcome in Christian leadership for the church represent a widening gap between the college and the church? Is there a difference between denominational and non-denominational colleges and universities on this assessment?

INTEGRATION IN PRESIDENTIAL LEADERSHIP

CCC presidents, past and present, were also asked, "How would you rate the overall impact of the CCC in helping you as a president to be a more effective advocate for the integration of faith and learning, on and off the campus?" Although all respondents indicated that the CCC had some impact in support of their presidential leadership and the majority (60.7 percent) rated the impact as "Significant," the average score was 4.43. Variations were evident with 40 percent of the presidents indicating that the CCC had less that "Significant" impact. The differences may be related to the individual initiative of the presidents. This observation is reinforced by the fact that past presidents rated CCC influence on their leadership as "Significant" while current presidents reported "Some Impact."

CCC IMPACT IN HIGHER EDUCATION

To gain a historical perspective on the purpose of the Consortium, past and present presidents were asked to review the forty years since its founding and rate its impact for the understanding, implementing, and advancing the integration of faith and learning in the sectors of higher education. Ratings of the presidents are:

	Mean Score:
On your campus?	3.93
In Christian higher education	3.82
In global higher education	3.07
In American higher education	2.96

Consistent with the foundational purpose of the CCC, the greatest impact came on the respective campuses of CCC colleges and universities, but with great variation. The responses for those who rated the impact as "Significant" (31.6 percent) were equal to those who gave a rating of "Some Impact" or less (31.6 percent). Even more variation is seen in the responses of the presidents to the impact of the CCC in Christian higher education. Median scores for this item show lesser "Significant" impact (15.8 percent) in Christian higher education, but stronger ratings for "Some Impact" or stronger (78.9 percent) for the overall scores. All scores drop off when it comes to rating the impact of the CCC in American higher education (57.9 percent rate "No" or "Little" impact) and in global higher education (47.4 percent rate "No" or "Little" impact). For the global sector, however, 26.3 percent gave the "Some Impact" rating to the CCC, most likely due to the global emphasis in recent years. The very limited impact of the CCC in American higher education poses a continuing challenge for the future of the faith-affirming and Christ-centered college and university.

PRIORITIES FOR THE FUTURE

If the "past is not yet over," no one has a better perspective on the future of the CCC than past and present presidents. Looking back upon forty years since the founding the Consortium, the final question of the survey tapped the experience and wisdom of the presidents by asking, "What do you consider the priority needs for advancing the integration of faith and learning for Christian colleges and universities in the future?" The results help define the expectations for today's and tomorrow's presidents in the academic arena.

Order of Priority:	Mean Score
1. *Infusing integration* into professional majors, graduate studies, urban and international experiences and online learning	3.93
2. *Assessing the educational outcomes* of integration as a Christian worldview, Christian character, Christian competence, and Christian servant-leadership	3.11
3. *Renewing the core* curriculum in the Christian liberal arts	3.00
4. *Understanding the history, theology, and philosophy* of the integrative concept	2.68
5. *Building faculty development programs* with a focus on the integration of faith and learning	2.29

Presidential respondents had difficulty in sorting out these priorities because they felt that all of them held high importance. When forced to make the choice, however, differentiation among the items comes clear. In support of the earlier findings in the survey, the infusion of integration into professional majors, graduate studies, international studies, urban experiences, and especially, online learning has highest priority.

At the other end is the surprising result regarding faculty development with a focus upon the integration of faith and learning. Presidents feel as if faculty development is a continuing strength to which CCC colleges and universities already give careful attention. Their rating gains support by a random survey conducted by Samuel Joeckel and Thomas Chesnes among faculty at CCCU schools.[1] 94.7 percent of the respondents strongly agreed or somewhat agree with the statement "I have a good idea of what is meant by the phrase 'the integration of faith and learning.'" 83.8 percent strongly agreed or somewhat agreed with the statement, "It is not difficult for me to integrate faith and learning in my discipline." With the strength of these responses from a random survey of CCCU schools, one can infer that the concept is at least as strong in CCC institutions where intentional development has been emphasized for the past thirty-two years.

OVERVIEW OF FINDINGS

Summarizing the findings of the survey as a whole, a profile of integration in CCC colleges and universities can be drawn. On the basis of the presidents' ratings, we can conclude that the integration of faith and learning is a strong and pervasive influence in the academic climate of these institutions. Standing out are the special strengths of integration in the co-curricular chapel and student development programs along with the core curriculum in the Christian liberal arts. Complementing these strengths are the key areas of faculty development with a focus on integration—recruiting, tenure, promotion, and orientation. Of lesser strength, but still influential, is the faculty understanding of the history, theology, and philosophy of the integrative concept and the assessment of student outcomes especially related to Christian character in lifestyle and Christian competence in career.

CCC presidents are also realistic about weaknesses in key areas of institutional development related to the integration of faith and learning. In each of the areas of strength, there is a counterbalancing weakness that calls for attention. In curriculum development, the need is for integration in new delivery systems, such as online learning; in instructional methods, faculty innovation on integrative approaches deserves attention; in faculty development, mentoring and rewarding faculty for integration understanding and application has real merit; and in assessment of student outcomes, the weakness of Christian leadership for the church stands out.

A similar balance of strength and weakness is evident in the responses of the presidents regarding the impact of the CCC in support of their leadership for the integration of faith and learning. Past presidents saw CCC support as "Significant" while current presidents sensed only "Strong" impact. The CCC impact in the multiple sectors of higher education shows

1. Joeckel and Chesnes, *The Christian College Phenomenon*, 356–357

even greater variation. As would be expected, the greatest impact of the CCC came on individual college campuses followed by its influence in Christian higher education. In American and global higher education, however, the impact was limited and reflected in the lowest mean scores for the whole survey.

Finally, in setting an agenda for the future, the CCC presidents put top priority on infusing the integrative concept into curricular areas reaching into professional studies, graduate programs, off-campus experiences, and new delivery systems, such as online learning. Lowest priority for the future went to faculty development focused on the integration of faith and learning. In between, they called for attention to renewing the core curriculum, assessing student outcomes, and understanding the scholarly roots of the integrative concept.

COLLEGIAL COMPANY

If I were to do the CCC presidents' survey again, I would ask them, "What has been the value of CCC presidential relationships for you personally?" Part of their annual meeting time is set aside for personal retreat and collegial sharing among the presidents and their spouses. As a participant in the meeting for ten years my wife, Janet, and I can to attest to the bonus of the experience.

A college or university presidency is a lonely job, even in a Christ-centered institution. No one understands what this means without being in the role. My first presidency coincided with a surge in cell groups as a means for spiritual discipline and renewal. Four members of my administrative team organized a small group for prayer and Bible study. At their urging, I attended one of the meetings. The leader began by saying that confidential accountability was the intent of the group with the members sharing things that not even their wives could know. I felt trapped because the presidency includes moments of private counsel for decisions that cannot involve staff members who have invested interest in the outcomes. Later on, I had to dismiss two members of the group.

In our second presidency, my wife and I were at the age where couples connect around children and enjoy social relationships. We were naturally drawn to faculty couples of the same age and interest. All went well until I presented a budget that called for cuts based upon strategic planning priorities. One of the faculty members with whom we socialized had lesser cuts than other members of his department. Our relationship became the fuse for igniting controversy and charging favoritism. A wrenching decision had to be made. We remained friends with the couple, but limited our association to formal occasions.

In our third presidency, we were reunited with long-time friends and classmates on the faculty who immediately wrapped us up in love. Again, an invitation came to join a small prayer group of faculty with whom we could share our presidential burdens and receive their support. They didn't understand when I tried to explain that presidents can have colleagues but not confidants within the institution, even when they are brothers and sisters in Christ.

Out of these experiences, I developed guidelines for counseling with presidents and other chief executive officers.

Every president needs a confidant with whom he or she can speak about anything, including the confession of sin and power of temptation. This must be a person who has no vested interest in the institution and is willing enter into a mutual covenant of confidence. Dr. Lloyd Olgivie and I entered into such a relationship after we worked together on writing *The Communicator's Commentary.*

Every president also needs a group of peers dedicated to Bible study, prayer, and spiritual growth. The group may be from within the institution, but it is still preferable to have that relationship with an outside group. During our time in Seattle, I met once a month with a small group of business, political, and judicial leaders. An unforgettable moment came during one of those meetings when a Justice of the Washington State Supreme Court told how our Bible study on the woman taken in adultery led him to a decision of mercy for a convicted felon who had served his time with evidence of rehabilitation.

All presidents and their spouses especially need colleagues with whom they share the unique circumstances of executive leadership. There is no formal preparation for being the President, First Lady, or "First Laddy" on the Christian college or university campus. Even as I write, my wife Janet has an email asking about the role and responsibility of the president's spouse for trustees during their board meetings. The annual retreat of the CCC has developed into that kind of collegial resources for its presidents and spouses. Members know this is a setting when they can "take down their hair" without fear of broken confidence or inattention. Death, divorce, discipline, and dismissal have all been aired over the history of the meetings so that CCC presidents and spouses know a relationship that brings them back together even after retirement from their institutions. The "President's Club" might well be replicated as an invaluable resource for all of Christ-centered higher education.

REPRISE

The diverse threads of our story now come together into a tightly woven cord. From CCC history, presidential insights, and personal experience, we conclude that the CCC has met its founding purpose of advancing the integration of faith and learning as the defining mission and distinguishing character of the Christian college and university. Having the advantage of a personal relationship with all of the charter member presidents of the CCC and with most of those who have succeeded them, I can attest their unswerving commitment to the integrative concept. Furthermore, a close association with the presidents of the CCC over the years—Ed Neteland, Gordon Werkema, John Dellenback, Carl Lundquist, Tom England, and Stan Gaede—leaves no doubt about their leadership on behalf of the integrative process through the organization and institutions of the CCC. But, as we have noted several times, the idea of integration must be renewed in each generation of presidential leadership. To that agenda, we now turn.

17

Thrust for Today

INTEGRATION IN CHRIST-CENTERED HIGHER education is not a self-renewing process. Boards, presidents, and faculties in each new generation have individual and institutional responsibilities. Christian scholars must renew their commitment to integration in their teaching and through their research seek to bring some measure of transformational change in the heart of the academic body. Like Alexis De Tocqueville's "representative character" in American democracy, the individual scholar must be shaped by "inherited values on the one hand and the challenges of the expanding frontier on the other."[1] Biblical convictions and new knowledge will always be the challenge for the Christian scholar.

At the same time, the call to commitment goes beyond the individual to the institution. Scholars must join with trustees and presidents in creating what Robert Bellah calls "moral ecology" or the "web of moral understandings and commitments that tie people together in community."[2] Applied directly to the Christ-centered college and university, the same commanding truth that integrates faith and learning in the classroom makes all things whole for the campus community, whether in the curricular, co-curricular or extra-curricular climate. The order is large and the task is not easy, but if we are who we say we are, the pervasive influence of our Christ-centered commitment will be present in every facet of our

1. Bellah, et al., *Habits of the Heart*, 39.
2. Ibid., 335.

individual and institutional being. Each generation has its work cut out in an agenda of renewal that carries forward inherited values into the expanding frontier.

To insure our heritage and address the new frontier, ten fundamental questions need to be asked and answered by boards, presidents, deans, and faculty leaders of Christian colleges and universities, especially in pivotal times such as strategic planning sessions, accreditation self-studies, and presidential transitions. The moral ecology of a Christ-centered campus depends upon each new generation giving affirmative answers to these ten questions.

1. *Is Jesus Christ, "in whom all things hold together," identified as the commanding truth for the integration of faith and learning?* During the past fifty years Christian colleges and universities have advanced from being "faith-defending" to "faith-affirming" institutions. We must go one more step and identify the faith that we affirm. Biblical revelation, historic creeds, sound reason, and personal experience make it clear. Jesus Christ must be "the" perspective for learning if we are identified as "Christ-centered" and if we have the affirmation of a "commanding truth" in which faith and learning come together in the integrative process. Anything less buries the seeds of defection just beneath the surface of the academic process where they are ready to sprout if watered by the mental reservations of a new generation.

2. *Is Christ-centered integration of faith and learning specifically affirmed in our vision, mission, and strategic planning statements?* Lewis Carroll, in *Alice in Wonderland*, lets the Cheshire Cat say it for us, "If you don't know where you are going, any road will get you there." Educators know that learning outcomes are never achieved without learning objectives. If the integration of faith and learning is the primary reason for the existence of the Christian college and university, it must be stated pointedly at the front edge of our vision, mission, and strategic planning documents. Forget the internal criticisms about the phrase becoming a "shibboleth." If Christian higher education is to carry its case into the academic marketplace, let it be led by the claim "to integrate biblical revelation centered in Christ and human learning centered in the liberal arts." Giveaways on faith and learning objectives to gain academic standing, marketing clout, political power, capital campaigns, or financial aid to students will invariably dilute the impact upon student outcomes. Strategic plans that spell out our vision and mission especially need the driving force of a precise statement on integration as its pervasive guide. Marketing plans for attracting students

should avoid cute little ploys and come directly to the experience of integrative teaching and learning. All other incentives for attending the Christian college are secondary to this experience. Even if a student chooses the Christian college for the wrong reason, it is our obligation to do the right thing. When all is said and done, it will be the integration of faith with learning, living, and serving to which our alumni will give testimony.

3. Is the integration of faith and learning front and center in the professional qualifications, nurturing plans, and performance standards for presidential leadership? As we have seen in the organization of the CCC and the spinoff of the CCCU, presidents have taken the lead in advocating and advancing the integration of faith and learning. Because the future is also in his or her hands, the president's task description should include the expectations that he or she will champion the understanding, communication, and implementation of integration in every phase of campus life. Further, we expect that the president's recommendations for board policy, strategic plans, curricular offerings, administrative and faculty appointments, and funding campaigns will be consistent and conducive to the integrative concept. Most important of all, we expect that the president will personally model integration in thinking, living, and serving Christianly.

4. Is the integration of faith and learning prominent in our plans for the ongoing education of our board members? As strange as it may seem, Christian college and university boards are least comfortable with academic matters and least knowledgeable in understanding the integration of faith and learning. Their commitment to the concept is firm, but the tendency is to defer to the administration and the faculty because it is assumed that knowledge and implementation belongs to the scholars. If, however, we accept the premise that integration is the reason for the existence of the Christian college and university, the assurance of its integrity rests with the board. The concept is important enough to be included specifically in the by-laws of the corporation as one of the responsibilities of a board member.

As we have already noted, studies have shown that a difference between effective and ineffective boards is the ability of the members to answer the question, "What is our mission?" To be fully effective, board members of a Christian college or university should also be able to answer the question, "What is our distinctive?" Another sixty-second elevator speech comes to mind, but it will never be given without a plan for trustee development that involves knowledge and understanding of the history, theology, and philosophy of integrative learning.

Orientation of new trustees is the starting point for an understanding of integration. Even if the trustee is a graduate of a Christian college or university where integration is stressed, there is always room for review. The orientation packet, for instance, should include a readable book on integration that can become the basis for discussion in the formal orientation session. Sources in the field are plentiful, and of course, the little classics of Holmes' *The Idea of the Christian College* or John Stott's *Your Mind Matters* are readable starters. Trustee reading, then, can be backed up by faculty presentations on integrative learning and visits to classrooms to see the process in practice.

Trustees will also give strong support to the president as an advocate for the integration of faith and learning. Assuming that the president's task description puts high priority on integration, trustees will want to follow that expectation into performance reviews. Is the president an advocate for understanding, communicating, and implementing integration in every phase of institutional life? Do the president's recommendations for strategic plans, curriculum offerings, faculty appointments, new initiatives, and funding campaigns advance integration? Does the president personally model integration in thinking, living, and serving Christianly? As we have seen in the history and the survey of the CCC, presidential leadership is the indispensable ingredient in keeping the integration of faith and learning alive and well.

5. Are faculty development plans from recruitment to retirement designed to understand, nurture, and reward the integration of faith and learning? CCC presidents rated faculty development lowest on their agenda for the future. If our earlier conclusion about the history of Christian higher education is correct, it should be at the top of the list. Three reasons back up this conclusion. First, integration is *spiritual.* Unless a faculty member is personally committed to Jesus Christ as Savior and Lord, there is no centering point by which all things hold together. Deep-seated spiritual commitment should be in the qualifications for faculty positions in Christ-centered colleges and spiritual formation should be an ongoing expectation for faculty development. But, none of us grows spiritually in solitude. The ethos of the campus community should be lifting all of its members on the rising tide of spiritual growth. At Seattle Pacific University, for instance, administration, faculty, staff, and students are invited to participate in a "Journey through God's Word," an online program called *Lectio: A Guided Bible Study.* Weekly commentaries, led by members of the religion faculty, will take the readers through most of the Bible in a four-year period. Chapel, Bible studies, and group discussions are planned around the commonly-read scripture and creates a campus-wide climate conducive to teaching the integration of faith and learning.

Next, integration is *intellectual*. By the very nature of scholarship, faculty members possess inquiring minds that explore options, test assumptions, live with ambiguity, and demand proof for conclusions. Or, as one president put it, "Faculty are people who think otherwise." We would not want it any other way, but unless these intellectual virtues are grounded in the confidence that the Word is God's inspired, authoritative, and final revelation coupled with the God-breathed Spirit, shaky faith will crumble before philosophies that contradict or undermine this truth. Academic freedom is not compromised by this position. Rather, it is confirmed by the willingness of Christian scholars to explore all truth from a biblical perspective, daring to say "I don't know" to unanswered questions, eager to continue research into those questions, and letting faith fill in the gaps of the unknowns.

Finally, integration is *incarnational*. As our survey has shown, the farther we get from the core of our Christian liberal arts curriculum, chapel services, and residential experiences, the more difficult it is to infuse integration into the student learning experience. Face-to-face interpersonal relationships between faculty and students represent the continuation of incarnational ministry when "the Word becomes flesh."

Christian higher education has no room for "giving-getting" contracts in which a faculty members gives only as much as he or she gets. Total self-giving in the Spirit of Christ, even sacrifice, is the only justification for a faculty position in the Christian college or university. All of its claims are diluted, even nullified, if its faculty members are not fully committed to Christ, to the student as a whole person, and to the integration of biblical faith and human learning within the context of their scholarly field. To date, we have relied on natural networks to bring prospective faculty to our attention. Candidates are often graduates of Christian colleges and universities or colleagues of Christian scholars who have them on their radar screen. As good as these networks are, we must become more intentional about identifying and recruiting faculty for the future. Profiles for prospects and procedures for interviews should have specific expectations about integration as a personal and scholarly interest related to the position. Although prospects cannot be expected to be lay theologians, a level of biblical literacy is essential to the integrative process. Prior to being hired, a candidate may be asked to present a lecture before his faculty peers integrating biblical faith with a subject in his or her discipline. Once appointed, faculty with whom we are sharing a life investment deserve the nurturing relationship of a senior faculty mentor and ongoing opportunities for departmental, institutional, and CCCU workshops dedicated to the integration of faith and learning. Likewise, in each stage of faculty advancement from promotion in rank to tenure in position, integration should be central to the process. Simply put, everything is at stake in the faculty of a Christ-centered college or university.

6. *Is the integration of faith and learning in the core curriculum of the Christian liberal arts being renewed for changing times while continuing to cultivate the intellectual skills of liberal education?* The Christian liberal arts curriculum that is required of all students is also the intellectual center for the integration of faith and learning. Periodically, this curriculum needs to be reviewed by the faculty in order to assure its continuing strength and relevance. Erosion of its strength can take place when professional demands override required courses, elective courses can be chosen as options, professors prefer to teach in their specialties, and when integration gives way to information. Eventually, the result is a return to a "distributive" curriculum offered in cafeteria style. Without a cohesive core of integrative learning experiences, neither intellectual skills nor Christianly outcomes will be achieved in Christian higher education. Furthermore, a static curriculum, even in the Christian liberal arts, is no match for the dynamic changes that are taking place in our society today.

The integration of biblical revelation and human learning goes hand in hand with the outcomes of liberal learning. In the report by the Association of American Colleges and Universities, entitled *Liberal Education Outcomes* (2005), widespread agreement is given to the liberal education outcomes: (a) knowledge of human culture and the natural world through courses in the humanities, physical and social sciences, mathematics and arts; (b) intellectual and practical skills in written and oral communication, inquiry, critical and creative thinking, quantitative and information literacy, teamwork and the integration of learning; and (c) individual and social responsibility including civic responsibility and engagement, ethical reasoning, intercultural knowledge and actions, and propensity for lifelong learning. Special attention is given to a structure of experiences that begin with freshman orientation, learning contracts, and ongoing assessment continuing through focused studies in major and minor fields, with cap-stone experiences focused upon advanced integration in the student's chosen field of study.[3]

The AACU model is ideal for the Christian liberal arts because its outcomes are compatible with Christ-centered integration at every point. The temptation for presidents to expand with new programs and delivery systems and the desire of faculty to advance their reputation for scholarship in their respective fields must not make the core curriculum in the Christian liberal arts an academic stepchild. It sets the tone as well as the text for the distinctive character of the Christ-centered college and university.

At the same time, a false dichotomy must not be drawn between the core curriculum in the Christian liberal arts and professional studies. The outcomes of liberal learning in order to think, live, and serve Christianly must be infused throughout the whole curriculum of the Christ-centered college or university. One way to insure this connection is to identify the base of liberal arts in every professional discipline. For instance, when the School of Business and Economics was established at Seattle Pacific University in 1977, grounding in the liberal arts discipline of economics became part of the identifier for the School and the foundational requirement for business students. In most universities, School of Business students had to go to the School of Arts and Sciences to get a course in economics. The same was true for courses in ethics. With equal intent, economics and ethics were "mainstreamed" through the offerings of the new School.

7. *Is chapel the vital center where integrative influences come together and move outward throughout the campus community?* CCC presidents, past and present, give chapel the highest rating for integration in their institutions. As noted earlier, when Elton Trueblood visited Christian liberal arts colleges, he inquired first about the status of chapel. From the answer, he said that he could assess the extent to which the college was fulfilling its Christian purpose, not just spiritually, but intellectually as well. Trueblood saw the sad history of Christian higher education unfold before his eyes as he visited college after college where cathedral-like structures stood like relics of a forgotten past and deans of the chapel were carried along like excess baggage. CCC colleges and universities, of course, are different, but not without perennial struggles to keep chapel as a vital, integrative center for community life on the campus.

3. AACU, *Liberal Education Outcomes*, 200.

As a former CCC president and chapel speaker at more than one hundred Christian college campuses over a period of fifty-five years, I have lived with all of these questions myself. Is the purpose of chapel spiritual, intellectual, or both? Is it primarily for preaching or teaching? Should chapel be compulsory or optional? Should chapel credit be required for graduation? Why don't the faculty attend? Will the worship be traditional, contemporary, or blended? Should the dean of the chapel or campus chaplain have faculty status? After all of these questions have been asked, the final question is, "What is the purpose of chapel on the Christian college campus?" The answer is in our commitment to the integration of faith and learning.

In the history of the colonial college, chapel carried the prestige of being "the President's Course." Held in the morning prior to the start of classes, the president presided and spoke to open the scriptures, relate them to fields of human knowledge, apply this understanding to moral issues, and personally model integration for both students and faculty. We cannot return to those days, but we can capture the principles that made chapel the vital center for integration in the campus community. To begin, chapel must be rethought as the natural center for bringing together the curricular and co-curricular learning with a focus upon the integration of faith and learning. As such, its definition, programming and assessment will be consistent with and complementary to the total thrust of the Christian learning community.

Chapel is an opportunity to teach Christ-centered integration as it relates to worship in praise and proclamation, fellowship in confession and communion, and community in sacrifice and service. To achieve this level of significance, chapel must have the authority of the president's office and the personal attention of its holder. Otherwise, it will be an appendage of student development and a step-child to academic interests. This does not mean that the Dean of Chapel reports directly to the President, but it does mean that the President is directly involved in the planning, funding, and leading of chapel services. A presidential series of chapel addresses through the year, a regular schedule of times when the president presides over services, and a visible presence in chapel whenever the president is on campus are the symbols of leadership that will set the tone and assure the text for chapel as the cohesive center for the integration of faith and learning.

8. *Is integration a pervasive influence throughout the institution, especially in new initiatives for teaching and learning?* Christian colleges and universities have been in a growth cycle for the last thirty years or more.

Enrollments have increased at record speed, most often due to the introduction of new programs, such as professional majors, graduate studies, extension centers, degree completion courses, and online learning. With each of these new initiatives for growth has come the challenge to infuse the integration into the teaching-learning process. CCC presidents, past and present, recognize this challenge and have put it first on their agenda for the future. As we observed from our survey, the farther we get from the core curriculum of the Christian liberal arts the weaker the influence of integration. Whether it is the stringent requirements of graduate or professional studies, the market-driven expectations of extension and degree-completion programs, the limited personal connection of online learning or the frequent use of adjunct faculty to staff the new initiatives, the integration of faith and learning suffers. As already noted, when policies and programs are introduced that move the Christian college or university away from its core curriculum, its face-to-face teaching with full-time faculty, and its resources of chapel and residency, boards, and presidents must be gate-keepers for the integrative concept.

A special word is in order about the virtual world of cyber-learning. In their survey, CCC presidents put a premium upon the need to relate integrative principles and processes to graduate and professional studies, online and distant learning. The fact is that curriculum development has sped ahead of our thinking and planning for integration in these areas. Financial resources rather than educational philosophy often drive these decisions. Belatedly, then, we try to justify these choices with an overlay of integrative philosophy.

Meanwhile, the cyber-learning world is spinning with possibilities unlimited for the dissemination of information and the promise of knowledge. It is time to stop the mad rush to keep up long enough to ask the question, "How can we assure incarnational teaching for virtual learning?" Our claim for distinction based upon our commitment to integrate faith with learning, living, and serving will rise or fall with the answer. Boards and presidents must anticipate this question and faculties must answer it before plunging headlong into the cyber-world. Creative options will be required and, in some cases, Christ-centered colleges and universities may have to decide that certain delivery systems may be detrimental to integrative learning based on incarnational teaching. In any case, a Christ-centered educational philosophy must take precedence over a market-driven economic policy.

9. *Is the integration of faith and learning, living and serving evident in the increasingly diverse community of the Christ-centered college and university?* By social trends and policy decisions, Christian colleges and universities are becoming more diverse in gender, racial, and ethnic representation. In fact, the CCC and the CCCU have been commended for leadership initiatives in minority recruiting and racial reconciliation. As suggested in our survey of CCC presidents, the strength of integration in student development areas points to a "grace-filled" community of proclamation, fellowship, and service. Can we maintain this strength in a society where religious pluralism is challenging the fundamentals of our faith?

In their book *American Grace*, Robert Putnam and David Campbell find a growing polarity between older and younger generation of evangelical Christians, not just over social issues, such as abortion and homosexuality, but also over religious issues such as the absolute truth of Christianity, the need for evangelism, and the reluctance to assign good neighbors to hell. As Putnam and Campbell put it, "Devotion plus diversity, minus damnation, equals comity."[4] This, they contend is "America's grace."[5]

Diversity means more than getting along with each other. Christian colleges and universities must teach students how to live as devout Christians in a religiously pluralistic society that will mute the faith for the sake of harmony. Going back to a homogeneous community or vanilla campus is not an option. Rather than waiting for the issues of diversity to put the Christ-centered college or university on the defensive, boards, presidents, and faculty should be anticipating the consequences of policy decisions related to diversity and becoming proactive in their responses. Religious diversity is a reality coming out of a rapidly changing culture that may well be the acid test for our claim that integration is the distinctive character of Christ-centered education.

10. *Are the qualitative goals of integrating faith and learning achieved in the assessment of student outcomes for the Christ-centered college and university?* Accountability, especially from federal and state agencies, is on the rise throughout American higher education. Voluntary accrediting agencies, as well, are stressing student outcomes related to educational goals as evidence of quality. Broad brushstrokes of regulation are sweeping Christian colleges and universities into the same mix with public and proprietary institutions. While meeting these expectations, we cannot forget that

4. Putnam and Campbell, *American Grace*, 540.

5. Ibid., 550.

Christian higher education makes claims for qualitative learning outcomes beyond governmental regulations or accrediting standards. As designated in our survey, these claims include Christian character and lifestyle, Christian competence in career, Christian leadership in the culture, Christian worldview, and Christian leadership in the church. Past and present CCC and the CCCU leaders have recognized the importance of research in these areas, but the results are still limited.

Not that research into educational outcomes for Christian colleges and universities has been lax. Under the title *The CCY and the Moral and Spiritual Development of their Students: A Review of Research,* Charles Stokes and Mark Regnerus summarize the findings of researchers from the 1980s to 2009. After detailing the outcomes of studies in the areas of moral development, ethical values, character development, faith and spiritual development, religious practices, and moral behavior, they point forward to the future with this conclusion:

> Christian colleges appear to do the best job supporting student's spiritual and moral growth, but the evidence is far from conclusive, and . . . the standard doesn't seem very high. Future studies must pay careful attention to issues of selection by measuring precollege characteristics and comparing students enrolled in Christian colleges with similar students in secular universities. Additionally, thoughtful attention can be given to understanding those elements which are necessary and/or sufficient for morally supportive campus cultures to work.[6]

Prophetic words. As moral issues escalate in an increasingly secular culture, the price of tuition rises, and public opinion joins government agencies in demanding accountability from all institutions of higher education, the need for advanced research into the special claims of Christ-centered colleges and universities rises as well. To date, evidence that these claims are being fulfilled is largely anecdotal. In our advertising, Christian colleges and universities seem to be casting about for some distinctive feature that will set them apart from the mush of marketplace. In recent years, "transformation" has become the buzzword that carries the promise of change, not just intellectually and spiritually, but in Christian leadership for changing the world. While no one will argue with the bold and worthy goal of transformational change, we must back up our claims with evidence

---

6. Stokes and Regnerus, *The CCCU and the Moral and Spiritual Development of Their Students" A Review of Research,* 11.

of solid research. Popular polls, secular and religious, do not support these transformational claims. To the contrary, they continue to show serious disjuncture between the profession and practice of Christian believers. Little difference is found in the lifestyle, ethical behavior, consumer mentality, and entitlement expectations of evangelical Christians and their secular peers, particularly among young adults and the oncoming generation.

Are the graduates of Christ-centered colleges and universities different? An encouraging word comes from an alumni survey conducted in 2012 among church-related institutions and reported in *Christianity Today*:

> Sixty-five percent of alumni from church related institutions claimed their experience often included integration of values and ethics in classroom discussions while only 24 percent of alumni from the top 50 public schools indicated that they experienced such discussions; and 36 percent of alumni from church-related colleges said "their college experience helped them develop moral principles" while only 7 percent of alumni from the top 59 public schools claimed this outcome.[7]

While there is comfort in the comparison, further research is needed to determine whether or not Christ-centered institutions make a greater difference. At this time, we are not sure, but as the demands for accountability increase from parents of prospective students who will have to make deeper sacrifices for the values of Christ-centered education, we will either have to prove our point or reduce our claims. Qualitative and longitudinal research on student outcomes for Christ-centered colleges and universities, both in macro-studies for the whole sector and micro-studies for the individual institutions, must become a priority item on our agenda for today. Integration of faith and learning is just a hollow sound without the evidence of graduates who think, live and serve Christianly in the contemporary world.

When taken together, these ten questions penetrate into the very soul of the Christ-centered college or university. If we can answer these questions in the affirmative and back them up by the facts, the next generation will know that we have been true to our trust.

7. Glanzer, "The Missing Factor in Higher Education," 20.

18

Orbit for Tomorrow

OUT OF SIGHT IS out of mind. When we moved from Seattle Pacific University to the presidency of Asbury Theological Seminary, we changed neighborhoods, perhaps worlds. Our formal relationship with the Christian College Consortium came to an end. Then, in 1988, an unexpected invitation came to be the President of CCC. Richard Gross, President of Gordon College and Chair of the Board, presented what he called "A blank check" and asked me to fill it in. Needless to say, this was the offer of a lifetime. Nothing could be more attractive at the moment because I was in the tightening vice between the Seminary Board of Trustees' mandate to establish the E. Stanley Jones' Center for World Missions and Evangelism and faculty reluctance to share their scarce resources for the new venture. Although I inherited the issue, my predecessor's war had become my war. Moreover, the invitation from the CCC reawakened my passion for integrating faith and learning at the collegiate level. What would I do? God had called me to Asbury and now I heard the call to the CCC. In quiet desperation, I called my close friend and colleague, George Brushaber, President of Bethel College and a member of the Executive Committee for the CCC. Even though he wanted me to accept the CCC invitation, he heard my plight, framed it in a spiritual context, and concluded, "God not only calls us, but he also releases us. Do you feel released from your call to Asbury?" His question haunted me for days until I reread Isaiah's call from God to which he answered, "Here am I, send me." Isaiah got more than he bargained for. God's call was to tell the truth to people who would not listen, understand, or respond to the prophet's message. No wonder Isaiah pled," For how long, O Lord?" God answered with words we do not want to hear. Predicting the total devastation of Judah and the shame of Babylonian exile with only a seed of hope in the old stump of a remnant from the dregs of society, God asks Isaiah to be faithful to his call even though he will never see that seed of hope come to fruition in Jesus Christ. There was no escape from the message for me. Just as clearly as I had been called to Asbury Theological Seminary, I had to be released from that call in order to accept the presidency of the Christian College Consortium. What a shock to my spiritual system! As an ambitious man who had spent a lifetime reaching up to the next rung on the ladder, God wanted to teach me the lesson of faithfulness. Try as I might, I could not get a sense of release from my call to the Seminary. Peace came only when I prayed the prayer of the Bishop Lord Fenelon,

> Smite me or heal me,
> Depress me or build me up.
> I adore Thy purposes,
> Though unknown to me.[1]

Still, the push and pull of a "win-win" situation tugged at me until I called to decline the invitation. Two years later, his purposes became known. Asbury received the largest grant ever given to a free-standing seminary in American history. Twenty years after that grant and in my retirement years, Ira Galloway, Chair of the Association of Theological Schools Board at the time of the grant, called to say that no one else could have shepherded the gift through all the twists and turns along the way.

Out of the greatest spiritual lesson I ever learned came another chapter in the making of a movement in Christ-centered higher education. While weighing the invitation from the CCC, I went into retreat and spun a vision for the next level of impact for the integration of faith and learning. Now, this vision blends with the momentum of our movement to launch our thoughts into a new "orbit for tomorrow."

ASSURING ACADEMIC QUALITY

Throughout this book I have stressed again and again my strong conviction that self-regulation is the best protector of freedom for the Christian college

---

1. *The Homiletic Review*, 538

and university. Throughout the second half of the twentieth century and into the early decades of the twenty-first century, federal and state regulations have been picking at our independence like a flock of ducks. During my career, the threat peaked with the establishment of the Department of Education during the Carter administration. My concerted opposition to the DOE led to my nomination as Secretary of Education in the Reagan Cabinet, with a pledge to dismantle and reconstruct the Department. Today, the DOE still exists, and with increased power and money, it is sending tentacles of regulation into every phase of elementary, secondary, and higher education, whether public or private. The self-regulation of voluntary accrediting agencies, regional and professional, is not exempt. Through the conduit of the Council on Postsecondary Education, where I served as a board member, there will be added pressures to conform on academic, economic, and even social issues. Christ-centered higher education must anticipate these threats rather than reacting to them. One way to preserve the distinction we claim is to consider voluntary self-regulation for assuring the quality of the integration of faith and learning in our institutions. In chapter 17, I proposed a list of questions based on a holistic approach to integration throughout the institution. These are questions that will never be asked by federal agents or accrediting teams unless we ask them first and answer them by voluntary self-regulation. One approach might be to develop a self-assessment tool that Christ-centered colleges and universities could use to complement regional and professional accrediting standards, review the status of integration throughout the institution, and even invite colleagues from other schools to participate in the exercise. Another step might be to use the instrument for research studies on integration in member schools of the CCCU connection. Perhaps the time might also come when a similar instrument could serve as a guide for self-study on the integration of faith and learning for voluntary accreditation among Christ-centered schools. If past patterns hold, presidents, deans, and faculty members of Christian colleges and universities are ready volunteers to serve on accrediting teams for other institutions. With the distinctive character and quality of the Christ-centered college and university at stake in the integrative process, why not assume that the same spirit of voluntarism would be shown for serving on visiting teams to sister schools? All parties would learn from each other, the network of Christian higher education would be strengthened, and the distinctive of the Christ-centered college or university would be affirmed with the note of freedom. The precedent has already been set by the leadership of Senator Mark Hatfield and Charles Colson as they championed the establishment of the Evangelical Council of Financial Accountability in 1979, when economic abuses of some ministries threatened to smear the whole non-profit evangelical sector. As ECFA membership through voluntary self-regulation has strengthened the financial credibility to Christian ministries, we may need a similar process for reinforcing the academic quality of our Christ-centered colleges and universities, specifically in our focus upon the integration of faith and learning. It could be another way to demonstrate our mission, differentiate our identity, and get ahead of the broad broom of governmental policies and regulations.

EMPOWERING CHRISTIAN SCHOLARSHIP

One of the frustrating questions that will not go away is, "How can Christian scholars gain recognition in the academic community?" Various answers have been given. Carl F. H. Henry carried the hope of a Christian university until the day of his death. In the 1960s, he led a group of Christian educators in the establishment of the Institute for Advanced Christian Studies with the thought of identifying prominent Christian scholars in colleges and universities across the country, inviting them to membership, and finding ways to encourage their work by research grants and publications. Later, in the 1980s, Nathan Hatch and Joel Carpenter started the Evangelical Scholarship Initiative at the University of Notre Dame, with the specific purpose of "stimulating and supporting" evangelical scholarship through research grants, conferences, and publications. Funding from the Pew Foundation gave impetus to the idea through significant grants for the Pew Evangelical Scholars and Pew Younger Scholars programs. Coming alongside these initiatives was the *Christian Scholars Review*, a refereed journal dedicated to publishing the work of Christian faculty with focused interest on the integration of faith and learning. From those touch points, uncounted efforts have been made at individual institutions, such as the Baylor Institute for Christian Studies, and by disciplinary areas, such as the Society for Christian Economists, to create a climate of strength for Christian scholars in the academic community. Also, the Council of Christian Scholarly Studies was formed as an umbrella organization for the many societies of Christian scholars in specific disciplines. Members of the CCSS include scholarly societies in such fields as economics, mathematics, political science, theater arts, visual arts, literature, history, philosophy, and theology. As noble as these efforts are, they tend to be as fragmented as Christian colleges were in the mid-twentieth century. Except for a few instances where substantial funding grants were received, their impact has been limited. For those of us in Christian colleges and universities, it often seems as if these efforts are guided by the tacit assumption that evangelical Christian scholars serving in prestigious institutions had achieved the highest level of professional esteem at the point of penetration for impact in secular thought. Professors in Christian colleges and universities are not without honor, but at a lesser level. If such an assumption exists, it is grossly wrong. The fact is that the intellectual fire power of professors in Christian colleges and universities is an untapped resource for advancing the cause of Christian higher education, not just in the ministry of the church, but in the broader academic community and the public domain as well. If we believe that the integration of faith and learning defines the character of the Christ-centered institution, we need to recognize the scholars who carry that distinction in their research, teaching and service. As James Davison Hunter said it so precisely, "Inquiry, scholarship, and learning with awareness of the goodness of God's created order is a discovery of what is truly higher in higher education."[2]

It is time to revisit the idea of an Academy of Christian Scholars as an international network that gives highest esteem in the academic community to Christian scholars *who excel in advancing the integration of faith and learning,* whether in the Christian college or the secular university. A charter class of distinguished scholars would set the standards for membership. Admission to the Academy would be highly selective with classes of scholars nominated and chosen by their peers each year. Criteria for selection would include significant contributions of research and publication in their discipline, effective classroom teaching, mentoring of younger professors, and personal modeling, all in the context of integrating faith and learning. Members could be named as "Fellows" of the Academy with "Senior Fellow" status for retirees. For the first time, then, Christian scholars within the Christian college and university sector would be given the status they deserve, recognized in the academic community according to its highest standards, and empowered as a viable network representing Christian higher education. Charges of elitism would undoubtedly be leveled at the idea, but the advantages far outweigh this criticism. One only needs

2. Hunter, *To Change the World,* 254.

to think of the incentive for younger Christian scholars who are called to teach in Christian colleges. The potential for recognition as a member of the Academy would be an added reason to consider the Christian college and another stimulus for their scholarship once the career decision is made.

ASSESSING SUSTAINABILITY

If higher education has a besetting sin, it is the tendency to splendid isolation. In what is euphemistically called the "Ivory Tower," academic scholars advance theories, research ideas, teach students, and publish journals in the protective climate of academic freedom. The expectation is that "input" from homes, churches, and lower schools will produce prospective students with fertile minds and the "output" will be college graduates who will positively influence our primary institutions in order to keep the cycle turning over and over again. Because of this interdependence, higher education needs to accept greater responsibility for articulating with its "input" and accounting for its "output."

Christian colleges and universities are subject to the same temptation, but not without sacrificing the integrity of their redemptive mission. Secular higher education may be notorious for failing to articulate with secondary higher education and equally notorious for letting the chips of the college experience fall where they may. Christian colleges and universities do not have that luxury. In the review of research that we have already cited under the title, *The CCCU and the Moral and Spiritual Development of Their Students,* there is a forward-looking recommendation with profound implications. In short, Christian higher education is inseparably linked with the Christian home and Christian church.[3] Although further research is needed, Christian higher education is part of a "cycle of sustainability" that begins with the efficacy of the Christian home complemented by the Christian church in the moral and spiritual development of young people who can gain the most from the Christian college and university experience. Even if a Christian college or university admits non-Christian students, it must have a critical mass of Christian students to fulfill its mission of integrating faith and learning with the goal of graduates who think, live, and serve Christianly. At this point, the weight of responsibility shifts to the quality of the educational environment in the school itself. As the CCCU

3. Stokes and Regnerus, *The CCCU and the Moral and Spiritual Development of Their Students,* 11.

report suggests, "liberal-arts curriculum, service learning, low density, diverse peer networks, frequent interactions with faculty, and various specific interventions (such as courses or seminars specifically addressing morality) all contribute to growth in students' moral development."[4] While not specifically stated, this list highlights the potency of communal strength in the Christian college and university. When curricular and co-curricular climates reinforce each other, Christian higher education is at its best. But, how intentional are we about nurturing the Christian home as our lifeline into the future? In the past, we used to joke about woman students enrolling in college for the "Mrs. Degree," but there is an element of truth in the quip that we cannot deny. The basis for the Christian family is still, "Marry me, marry my family, marry my God." A biblical theology of the Christian family should be in the curriculum of Christian higher education. We could also add, "Marry my church." Hence, the question, "How intentional are we about nurturing the Christian church as our lifeline into the future?"

Church leaders must address this question. As our survey shows, CCC presidents rate "Christian leadership for the church" weakest for the influence of integration among student outcomes. Is this continuing evidence that the relationship between the college and the church is still an issue that needs to be addressed? Because the church has it own identity crisis in the push and pull between established denominations and independent megachurch movements, what is the "church" for which the colleges are expected to prepare leaders? Rather than pushing past each other and ignoring the differences, college and church leaders must talk and keep talking. Their relationship is too crucial to the kingdom to be left to chance.

College leaders must also address this question. If chapels and spiritual life programs on campuses are cultivating a maverick church, criticizing denominations without a constructive alternative, or touting spirituality without religion, we are undercutting our lifeline for the future. Research to date backs up the concluding recommendation in the CCCU report,

> Finally, Christian colleges should consider how they can support the future church and family lives of their students—in addition to encouraging students' future vocational efforts. How well their alumni connect with local churches and raise their families could directly impact the health and survival of Christian universities in the future.[5]

4. Ibid., 4.
5. Ibid., 11.

Truth has been spoken with love. Christian higher education has excelled in its "outreach" to moral issues of global magnitude while taking for granted the life-giving resources of its "in-reach." Resisting the temptation of splendid isolation, we must pause, step back, review our priorities, and give special attention to the primary institutions of home and church on which we depend. Integration means that Christian higher education is a full partner in a system called the "Body of Christ," where articulation and accountability are virtues by which the whole Body "grows and builds itself up in love, as each part does its work" (Eph 4:16).

Further assessment of the critical factors related to the interaction of the home, church, and school should be high on our agenda for the future. Are students from Christian homes and churches better prepared morally and spiritually for the experience of Christian higher education? How does the curricular and co-curricular climate of the Christian college or university specifically support moral and spiritual development conducive to the Christian home and family as well as to vocational and societal leadership? What is the evidence that graduates of Christian colleges and universities lead in Christian homes, serve in Christian churches, and support Christian higher education to assure the continuing quality and growth of our schools? We can only imagine the full potential of the Christian family, Christian college, and Christian church working as one in the name and for the sake of Jesus Christ.

SERVING AT A RISK

"Service" defines and honors Christian colleges and universities. In the triad of teaching, research, and service that defines the purpose of American higher education our schools lead the way in preparing students for service. Colonial Christian colleges profoundly impacted our new nation by educating leaders in law, medicine, and ministry. When these professions became highly specialized at graduate levels and public universities entered the field, Christian colleges adopted teaching, nursing, and later, business as "service professions" meeting needs at the core of our culture. In these professions the moral issues are relatively clear, the risk is limited, the integration of faith and learning is a natural fit.

Without neglecting the core of our culture, we must take a serious look at kaleidoscopic change on the leading edge of our culture. New fields of learning are challenging Christian colleges and universities. International law, human rights, global economics, ecology, neuroscience, cybernetics, social networking, and mass communications are just a few of these challenges. As of now, these fields are not interpreted as "service professions" within a Christian context. They fit the category of "risk professions" where Christian leadership is limited, moral issues are murky, and the integration of faith and learning is an open question. Yet, these are the professions that are shaping and reshaping the character of our culture. Christian colleges cannot remain on the sidelines. The passion that took the apostle Paul to points of penetration in the far reaches of the Roman Empire needs to be rekindled in the mission of the Christ-centered college and university. A generic or global approach will not do the job. Every Christian college and university needs to stimulate its entrepreneurial edge and adopt a front-edge discipline by which it will be known. Such fields as law, economics, and communications, for instance, are directly related to the liberal arts with extensions into specializations at a point of penetration into our post-Christian world.

No college or university can do it alone. Once again, through cooperative action, Christ-centered colleges and universities can become a creative network leading the way with high impact at the points of penetration into the character of our culture. To serve at risk on the precarious edge of our post-Christian world is the next order of business for Christ-centered higher education.

SHARING SCHOLARLY RESOURCES

Globalization is a word on the lips of every Christian college administrator and an accent in every strategic plan. Most often, however, globalization is conceived as a learning experience for students who must live in ethnically diverse communities and lead in an interconnected and interdependent world. As good as these efforts are, they tend toward what is called a "Mercator" map which shows the globe revolving around an enlarged picture of one nation, one community, or one institution. To put the magnified image of our local Christian college or university at the center of the global universe is a form of institutional self-centeredness that feeds on competition and denies cooperation. Christ-centered colleges and universities that claim a global perspective, especially in North America, have a responsibility to reach out and make every institution of Christian higher education a full partner in the body of Christ.

Christian higher education in North America is one of the richest resources for kingdom ministry in the twenty-first century. Billions of dollars are invested in facilities and endowments, millions of alumni and current students represent its potential for world impact, and multiplied thousands of faculty scholars bring the brightest minds in Christendom together. Globalization turns the spotlight on these unbelievably rich resources. Christian higher education in the two-thirds world is just the opposite. In the midst of one of the greatest spiritual revivals in Christian history and with the most desperate need for discipling millions of converts, the two-thirds Christian world is educationally impoverished. Christian colleges, universities, and seminaries subsist on financial margins with students eking out an existence and faculty laboring to make bricks with straw. Globalization means that Christian higher education in the Western world has a responsibility to share its richness with the rest of the world. Wahlburt Buhlmann's book, *The Coming of the Third Church*, comes back to convict us.[6] Buhlmann minces no words when he contends that spiritual awakening in the Western world will not come until we sacrificially share our resources with the Third Church of the global south. His book was written in 1977 and its prophetic call still waits to be answered.

The Council for Christian Colleges and Universities has taken the first step toward this goal by giving affiliate status to international Christian colleges, universities, and seminaries. At the 1989 Lausanne Conference on World Evangelization in Manila, I proposed the establishment of a global computer network for theological seminaries that would function as a tool for dialogue between theologians in North American seminaries and their colleagues in the two-thirds world. All of the technology is available to create the network and Asbury Theological Seminary with its new "smart campus" offered to serve as the nexus. Only the will to share is missing. Christ-centered colleges and universities in North America need to step up to our name. Where do we begin?

The simplest starting point is to follow the lead of schools that have developed a working relationship with a sister institution oversees. Computer links can instantly open a communication between the schools, sharing information relevant to Christian higher education, and letting professors begin a dialogue with colleagues in the same fields. Rather than exercising the old imperialist mentality of adopting an inferior sibling, the relationship should be defined as a mutual partnership because both schools have so

6. Buhlmann, *The Coming Third Church*, 13.

much to learn from each other. Public acknowledgment of the partnership on both campuses should become well known and personalized by mutual visits of leaders, leading to the possibilities of student and faculty exchange. One tangible example of sharing resources would be the provision for full access to the library and learning resources of the North American institution. Another would be the exchange of ideas regarding the integration of faith and learning in the classroom. If all of the member institutions in the CCCU had a relationship with an international partner, the globe could literally be woven into a network of interlocking relationships. At the global level, then, the accrediting criteria for the Christ-centered institution could be applied and the groundwork laid for a future World Congress on Christian Higher Education. The lift in morale for our international partners would alone be worth the effort.

A FINAL WORD

What happened to Carl Henry's dream for an "evangelical Harvard"? Multiple efforts to create a new institution or remake an existing institution with this visionary identity have come and gone. In the mid-1970s, a group of educational leaders were invited to a meeting to weigh the options for establishing a flagship university for evangelical Christianity in honor of Billy Graham. Resources were not the question, but when the pros and cons were on the table, the venture was abandoned. No small part of the decision involved Billy Graham's reluctance to have a university named after him. He loved ideas and loved to listen to scholars, but his call to be an evangelist and his humble spirit would not let his name be attached to an academic institution.

Providence has its own way of working out the wisdom of God. In the twenty-first century, we need to talk about creating educational systems more than building academic institutions. Breakthroughs in the media world are already creating a revolution in the delivery systems for higher education. While they may be a threat to the potency of the residential campus and the personalized classroom, they are also an opportunity for Christ-centered higher education to develop its creative edge in missional integrity and academic quality. The potential for making an impact upon the society and the secular academy through an overlapping global system is so much greater than the university that Dr. Henry envisioned. Most important of all, the same system has the potential for closing the gaps between faith and reason, education and evangelism, church and school, home and abroad when they become partners in fulfilling the Great Commission. When Kenneth Kantzer, Carl Henry's successor at *Christianity Today* reflected Carl Henry's unfulfilled dream, he wrote,

> Great ideas die hard, but it was not to be. Perhaps the idea was ill-advised. Augustine taught us a millennium-and-a-half ago that Christianity is best understood not high in an ivory tower, but in the roaring thoroughfares of real life. In the radical pluralism of the modern world, a thousand rays of light may penetrate better than a single beam from a lighthouse.[7]

In its highest and best sense, this is the ultimate aim for the integration of Christian faith and human learning.

7. Kantzer, "The Carl Henry That Might Have Been . . .," 15.

Appendix

Christian College Consortium President's Roster

1971 to Present

ASBURY COLLEGE (UNIVERSITY)

Dennis Kinlaw	1968–1981
Cornelius Hager	1981–1983*
John Oswalt	1983–1986
Dennis Kinlaw	1986–1991
Edwin Blue	1991–1992
Cornelius Hager	1992–1993*
David Gyertson	1993–2000
Paul Rader	2000–2006
William Crothers	2006–2007*
Sandra Gray	2007–Present

BETHEL COLLEGE (NOW UNIVERSITY)

Carl Lundquist	1954–1982
George Brushaber	1982–2008
James Barnes III	2008–Present

GEORGE FOX COLLEGE (UNIVERSITY)

David LeShana	1969–1982
Edward Stevens	1983–1997

David Brandt   1998–2007
Robin Baker   2007–Present

GORDON COLLEGE

Harold Ockenga   1969–1976
Richard Gross   1976–1992
Judson Carlberg   1992–2011
D. Michael Lindsay   2011–Present

GREENVILLE COLLEGE

Orley Herron   1970–1977
Richard Stephens   1977–1993
Robert Smith   1993–1998
V. James Mannoia   1999–2008
Edwin Blue   2008–2009*
Larry Linamen   2009–Present

HOUGHTON COLLEGE

Stephen Paine   1936–1972
Wilber Dayton   1972–1976
Daniel Chamberlain   1976–2007
Shirley Mullen   2007–Present

MALONE UNIVERSITY

Everett Cattell   1960–1972
Lon Randall   1972–1981
Gordon Werkema   1981–1988
Ronald Johnson   1988–1989*
E. Arthur Self   1989–1994
Ronald Johnson   1994–2007
Gary Streit   2007–2010
Wilbert Friesen   2010–2011*
David King   2011–Present

MESSIAH COLLEGE

D. Ray Hostetter	1964–1994
Rodney Sawatsky	1994–2004
Kim Phipps	2004–Present

SEATTLE PACIFIC UNIVERSITY

David McKenna	1968–1982
David LeShana	1982–1991
Curtis Martin	1991–1992**
Curtis Martin	1992–1994
E. Arthur Self	1994–1995
Philip Eaton	1995–1996**
Philip Eaton	1996–Present

TAYLOR UNIVERSITY

Milo Rediger	1965–1975
Robert Baptista	1975–1979
Milo Rediger	1979–1981
Greg Lehman	1981–1985
Jay Kesler	1985–2000
David Gyertson	2000–2005
Eugene Habecker	2005–Present

TRINITY INTERNATIONAL UNIVERSITY

Harry Evans	1964–1974
Kenneth Myers	1974–1995
Greg Waybright	1995–2007
Jeannette Hsieh	2007–2008*
G. Craig Williford	2009–Present

WESTMONT COLLEGE

John Snyder	1969–1971
Kenneth Monroe	1971–1972*
Lyle Hillegas	1972–1975

Ernest Ettlich	1975–1976*
David Winter	1976–2001
Stan Gaede	2001–2006
David Winter	2006–2007*
Gayle Beebe	2007–Present

WHEATON COLLEGE

Hudson Armerding	1965–1982
Richard Chase	1982–1993
Duane Litfin	1993–2010
Philip Ryken	2010–Present

CHRISTIAN COLLEGE CONSORTIUM

Edward Neteland	1971–1973
David McKenna	1973–1974*
Gordon Werkema	1974–1977
John Dellenback	1977–1981
Carl Lundquist	1981–1990
Thomas Englund	1990–2008
Stan Gaede	2008–Present

* Interim President
** Provost and Chief Executive Officer

Bibliography

Association of American Colleges and Universities. "Liberal Education Outcomes: A Preliminary Report on Student Achievement in College." Carnegie Corporation grant, New York, 2005.

Beebe, Gayle and John Kulaga. *Concept for a College.* Spring Arbor, MI: Spring Arbor University Press, 2005.

Bellah, Robert et al. *Habits of the Heart.* Berkeley: University of California Press, 1991.

————. *The Good Society.* New York: Knopf, 1991.

Boulding, Kenneth. *The Meaning of the Twentieth Century.* New York: Harper Colophon, 1965.

Brubacher, John S. and Willis Rudy. *Higher Education in Transition.* New York: Harper and Brothers, 1958

Buffet, Warren. "Oracle of Omaha." Online: http://www.investinganswers.com/50 WarrenBuffetQuotesInspireYourInvesting-2310.php.no.27.

Buhlmann, Wahlbert. *The Coming of the Third Church.* Maryknoll, NY: Orbis, 1977.

Burtchaell, James Tunstead. *The Dying of the Light: The Disengagement of Colleges and Universities from Their Christian Churches.* Grand Rapids: Eerdmans, 1998.

Crouzel, Henri. *Origen.* San Francisco: Harper and Row, 1985.

Dockery, David. *Renewing Minds.* Nashville: Broadman and Holman, 2007.

Eaton, Philip. *Engaging the Culture, Changing the World.* Downers Grove, IL: IVP Academic, 2011.

Franke, August. *Reform, Renewal and Revival: A Pastor's Vision.* VirtueOnline: January 17, 2009.

Glanzer, Perry. "The Missing Factor in Higher Education." *Christianity Today*, March, 2011, 18–23.

The Gregorian Institute of Benedictine College, Kansas. Blog posted on January 9, 2012

Harper, William Rainey. *The Trend of Higher Education.* Chicago: The University of Chicago Press, 1905.

Hatfield, Mark. *Between a Rock and a Hard Place.* Waco, TX: Word, 1976.

Heie, Harold and David Wolfe. *The Reality of Christian Learning: Strategies for Faith-discipline Integration.* Eugene, OR: Wipf and Stock, 2004.

Heine, Ronald. *Origen: Scholarship in the Service of the Church.* Oxford: Oxford University Press, 2010.

Henry, Carl F. H. "Evangelical Colleges as Faith-affirming Institutions." *Christianity Today*, September 10, 1965, 25–26.

Higher Education for American Democracy: A Report of the President's Commission on Higher Education. Six Volumes. New York: Harper and Brothers, 1947. (Best known as The Truman Commission.)

Hill, Alexander. *Just Business: Christian Ethics for the Marketplace*. Downers Grove, IL: IVP Academic, 2008.

Holmes, Arthur. *The Idea of a Christian College*. Grand Rapids: Eerdmans, 1975.

Hostetter, D. Ray, *Univeritas and Moral Excellence*. Lanham, MD: University Press of America, 2007.

Hunter, James Davison. *To Change the World: The Irony, Tragedy, and Possibility of Christianity in the Late Modern World*. New York: Oxford University Press, 2010.

Hutchins, Robert. "*The Great Books of the Western World*, History." Wikipedia: The Free Encyclopedia.

Jellema, William. *From Red to Black? Special Preliminary Report on the Financial Status, Present and Projected, of Private Institutions of Higher Learning*. San Francisco: Jossey-Bass, 1971.

———. *From Red and Black? The Financial Status of Private Colleges and Universities*. San Francisco: Jossey-Bass, 1973.

Joeckel, Samuel and Thomas Chesnes, eds. *The Christian College Phenomenon: Inside America's Fastest Growing Institutions of Higher Learning*. Abilene, TX: Abilene Christian University Press, 2012.

Kantzer, Kenneth. "The Carl Henry That Might Have Been . . ." *Christianity Today*, April 5, 1993, 15.

Litfin, A. Duane. *Conceiving the Christian College*. Grand Rapids: Eerdmans, 2004.

Lorentzen, Melvin. "Final Report on the Faith/Learning Institute." Consortium of Christian Colleges, 1972.

Malik, James. *The Two Tasks*. Westchester, IL: Cornerstone, 1980.

Mannoia, V. James, *Christian Liberal Arts: An Education that Goes Beyond*. Lanham, MD: Rowman and Littlefield Publishers, 2000

Marsden, George. *The Outrageous Idea of Christian Scholarship*. New York: Oxford University Press, 1997.

———. *The Soul of the American University: From Protestant Establishment to Established Nonbelief*. New York: Oxford University Press, 1994.

McGrath, Earl. J. "The Future of the Church-related College." *Liberal Education*, March, 1961, Vol. LVII, No. 1. 1971, 1–18.

McKenna, David. *Megatruth: Hi-truth for a Hi-tech World*. San Bernadino, CA: Here's Life Publishers, 1988.

———. "World Evangelization and Christian Higher Education: Strategy for the Future." Keynote address for Christian Higher Symposium at the World Congress on Evangelization, Lausanne, Switzerland, 1974.

Neibuhr, H. Richard. *Christ and Culture*. New York: Harper and Row, 1951.

Noll, Mark. *Jesus Christ and the Life of the Mind*. Grand Rapids: Eerdmans. 2011.

———. *Turning Points: Decisive Moments in the History of Christianity*. Grand Rapids: Baker, 2000.

Outler, Albert, ed. *John Wesley*. New York: Oxford University Press, 1964.

Parker, Percy Livingstone, ed. *The Heart of John Wesley's Journal*. New York: Fleming H. Revell, 1739.

Parsons, Talcott and Gerald Platt. *The American University*. Cambridge, MA: Harvard University Press, 1973.

Patterson, James, *Shining Lights: A History of the Council of Christian Colleges & Universities*. Grand Rapids: Baker Academic, 2001.

Peterson, Michael. *With All Your Mind: A Philosophy of Christian Education*. Notre Dame, IN: University of Notre Dame Press, 2001.

Putnam, Robert and David Campbell. *American Grace: How Religion Divides and Unites Us*. New York: Simon and Schuster, 2010.

Ramm, Bernard. *The Christian College in the Twentieth Century*. Grand Rapids: Eerdmans, 1963.

Reisman, David. *Constraint and Variety in American Education*. New York: Doubleday, 1958.

Ringenberg, William. *The Christian College: A History of Protestant Higher Education in America*. Grand Rapids: Eerdmans, 1984.

St. Olaf Self-Study Committee. *Integration in the Christian Liberal Arts College*. Northfield, MN: St. Olaf College Press, 1956.

Smith, Huston. *The Purposes of Higher Education*. Westport, CT: Greenwood Publishing Group, 1971.

Stokes, Charles E. and Mark D. Regenerus. *The CCCU and the Moral and Spiritual Development of Their Students: A Review of Research*. Department of Sociology, University of Texas at Austin, 2009

Stott, John R.W. *Your Mind Matters*. Madison, WI: Intervarsity, 1972.

Strachan, Owen Daniel. *Reenchanting the Evangelical Mind: Park Street Church's Harold Ockenga, the Boston Scholars, and the Mid-century Intellectual Surge*. PhD Dissertation, Trinity Evangelical Divinity School, Deerfield, IL., 2011.

Taking Values Seriously: Assessing the Mission of Church-Related Higher Education. Phase II—September 1997 through September, 2001. A Fund for the Improvement of Postsecondary Education sponsored project of the Council of Christian Colleges and Universities

Trigg, Joseph. *Origen*. London: Rutledge, 1998.

Trueblood, Elton. *A Place to Stand*. New York: Harper and Row, 1969.

———. *The New Man for Our Time*. New York: Harper and Row, 1970.

Van Duzer, Jeffery. *Why Business Matters to God (And What Still Needs to Be Fixed)*. Downers Grove, IL: Intervarsity, 2010.

Washington Higher Education Secretariat. Online: http://www.whes.org.

Werkema, Gordon. "Evaluating the Outcomes of Christian Liberal Arts Colleges and the Values in Christian Higher Education." Proposal to The Lilly Endowment, 1975.

———. Proposal to the CCC Executive Committee to establish the Christian College Coalition, 1976.

Wesley, John, Charles Wesley, and George Osborn. *The Poetical Works of John and Charles Wesley*, Volume VI. London: Wesleyan-Methodist Conference Office, 1870.

Wuthnow, Robert, *Christianity in the Twenty-first Century: Reflections on the Challenges Ahead*. New Haven: Yale University Press, 1996.